C000008702

ANDALUCÍA
& THE COSTA DEL SOL
POCKET GUIDE

Channel Crested STEAKS ♀ 100 m

DIAMANT Restaurant

BROOKLAWN ♀ 100 m

JOE'S BURGERS Restaurant

ARTS & CULTURE

Space disc... featuring...

A TO Z INFO

SHOPPI

Shopping aroun... be

GATE BRIDGE ♀ 100 m

📍 MAP   🔗 SHARE

LIKE

Sailing under the Golden Gate Bridge today, it is interesting to consider that engineers once thought it impossible to span the Golden Gate Strait at this point, because of the depth of the water (318ft/ 97 meters at its deepest point) and the powerful tidal rush.

The city authorized studies for a bridge in 1917, but it was 1933 before the first shovel turned under the gaze of master engineer Joseph B. Strauss (no relation to the famous waltz composer). Four years later the bridge opened, at a cost of \$35 million and the lives of 11 construction workers. Today the bridge

INSIGHT ⊙ GUIDES
SPAIN

≡

🔍

📄 INTRODUCTION

📖 EXPLOR

FLORIDA
This new edition of Insight Guide
Florida is a comprehensive full-colour
travel guide packed with inspiration
and information on everything
from colourful surf bars and

FRANCE
This brand new edition Insight Guide
to France features outstanding
full-colour photography plus 250 brand new
edition specially selected stunning
photographs and hand-picked
exploration of all the places to go

💲 $8.99

💲 $8.99

ST LUCIA Pocket Guide
St Lucia is one of the most luscious
islands, home to dramatic
features, beaches and a lively
Caribbean culture. New for 2015,
the redesigned Insight Pocket
Guides offer full-colour guide

💲 $8.99

💲 $8.99

Walking Eye
mobile app

Discover the world's best destinations with the Insight Guides Walking Eye app, available to download for free in the App Store and Google Play.

The container app provides easy access to fantastic free content on events and activities taking place in your current location or chosen destination, with the possibility of booking, as well as the regularly-updated Insight Guides travel blog: Inspire Me. In addition, you can purchase curated, premium destination guides through the app, which feature local highlights, hotel, bar, restaurant and shopping listings, an A to Z of practical information and more. Or purchase and download Insight Guides eBooks straight to your device.

TOP 10 ATTRACTIONS

GRANADA
Once the capital of the Moorish Nasrid dynasty, who celebrated their power by building the sublime hilltop palace, the Alhambra. See page 76.

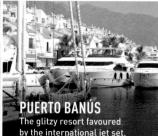

PUERTO BANÚS
The glitzy resort favoured by the international jet set. See page 42.

LA GIRALDA
Sevilla's most famous landmark was converted from a minaret into a bell tower. See page 65.

JEREZ DE LA FRONTERA
The heart of Spanish horsemanship and the home of sherry. See page 61.

DOÑANA NATIONAL PARK
One of the most important natural habitats in Spain. See page 63.

GIBRALTAR
An unmistakably British enclave on the Spanish coast. See page 44.

RONDA
Its ancient bullring is the birthplace of the modern bullfight. See page 56.

WHITE TOWNS
With their whitewashed houses and winding streets, these are a major feature of Andalucía. See page 58.

SANDY BEACHES
The Costa del Sol is blessed with miles and miles of them.

LA MEZQUITA
The magnificent Córdoban mosque was once the largest in the western Islamic world. See page 70.

A PERFECT TOUR

Day 1

Costa views

In Málaga, climb up to Castillo del Gibralfaro for fine views before visiting some of the city's other attractions. Head west from Málaga on the A7, following signs to the hilltop town of Mijas for late lunch while soaking up breathtaking views over the Costa. Descend to the coast and join the AP-7 southwest to Puerto Banús for a spot of designer shopping. Stroll round the port, relax over a cocktail and people watch at sunset.

Day 2

White towns

Take the A397 to Ronda. After exploring this spectacular town, suspended above an impressive gorge, round off the morning with lunch. Continue on the A374 to Sevilla, diverting to the white town of Olvera, where you can stretch your legs for a bit. Drive on to Sevilla on the A375/376 to put down roots for two nights.

Days 3-4

Sevilla

Soak up the atmosphere of the capital of Andalucía. With limited time, a walking tour (www.sevillawalking tours.com) provides a great introduction to the city. Then allow a bit more time to explore the city's top monuments; the Cathedral, La Giralda and the Real Alcázar. Round the day off with dinner followed by a flamenco show.

OF **ANDALUCÍA**

Day 6

Gibraltar

After breakfast in Cádiz's main square, head out on the A381: first through farmland and the city of Medina Sidonia and then through the Parque Natural de los Alcornocales, where you can take a forest walk among the cork trees. Continue on to Gibraltar, bearing in mind there may be queues at the border crossing.

Day 8

Costa chill

Take a well-earned rest with a day on the beach. Those keen on keeping more active can try the water sports on offer along this stretch, or play some golf.

Day 5

Cultural Cádiz

Make an early start down the AP-4 to Jerez de la Frontera, famous as the home of sherry and dancing horses. After sightseeing and lunch, set off on the same road for Cádiz. Considered Spain's oldest town, you will find an amalgam of architectural styles here. Take a bracing walk along the sea wall before dinner.

Day 7

Costa drive

Make an early start sightseeing on the Rock, including trying to spot the famous apes. Do some duty-free shopping, followed by lunch, before taking the coast road towards Estepona. Divert inland at Sabinillas on the A377 for the white village of Casares. Follow the MA8300 downhill to Estepona and join the Spanish for an early evening stroll along the esplanade before dinner in the old town. Stay at one of the many hotels or apartments along this stretch of beach.

CONTENTS

INTRODUCTION

Andalucía, Spain's southernmost autonomous community, is made up of eight provinces. Four of these are Huelva, adjoining Portugal and the Atlantic Ocean, and landlocked Sevilla, Córdoba and Jaén. The other provinces are strung along the southern coast of Spain between Gibraltar in the southwest and Almería to the east, encompassing parts of Cádiz, Málaga, Granada and Almería, and comprising the Costa del Sol.

For thousands of years, the people of the Costa del Sol, except when invaded or in times of war, went about their business oblivious to the concerns of the outside world. But in the last half of the 20th century that changed dramatically, when the Costa transformed itself from a collection of sleepy towns and fishing villages into the playground of the Western world. Surprisingly, the beaches on the Costa del Sol are not wide, with miles of yellow sand, as on the Atlantic coast. Instead, never far from the mountains and in some sections directly next to them, they are usually composed of a dull grey sand.

So what attracts millions of visitors from numerous countries every year? Air travel to the Costa is inexpensive and easy, with a wide choice of scheduled and charter flights. It is one of the liveliest and most cosmopolitan resort areas in the world, whose attractions range from swimming in the sea to skiing in the sierras. It has good beaches and the sun can be relied upon to shine nine days out of 10 almost all year round. Because the region is protected by an almost endless wall of mountains –the Sierra Nevada to the east of Málaga and the Serranía de Ronda to the west – it is spared the harsh, arid heat of the inland plateau. Temperatures in the summer rarely rise above 35°C (95°F). In addition, such a climate encourages an easy-going atmosphere;

Bolonia beach in the province of Cádiz

the local people still retain a gregarious, garrulous and generous nature, and tourists are made to feel very welcome.

WEST TO TARIFA

Málaga's international airport is the primary gateway to the Costa del Sol, which can be subdivided into two sections, west and east of Málaga. The more familiar image of the Costa del Sol is to be found to the west, where development reaches far back from the beaches. In the original tourist boom town of Torremolinos, high-rise hotels and squat apartment blocks loom above the waterfront promenade and the bustling back streets are lined with pubs, clubs, discos, chip shops, curry houses and other amenities familiar to British tourists. The apartment complexes around the marina at Benalmádena, however, are far more attractive.

Marbella, though, is very different. The original playground of the 1960s jet set and the upmarket showcase of the Costa del

Sol, it was first put on the map by Prince Alfonso von Hohenlohe in the 1950s. Today, movie stars, Arab potentates and other celebrities keep it in the news, though neighbouring Puerto Banús has emerged as the place to be seen. Magnificent yachts are moored in the marina, gourmet restaurants line the harbour, and sophisticated stores abound. Towards Estepona, hotels and apartment complexes diminish in number, as stretches of empty beach and green hillsides claim the landscape.

Continuing on, the familiar silhouette of the Rock of Gibraltar dominates the skyline. Across the bay, Algeciras is the gateway to North Africa, just across the Strait of Gibraltar. There are even better views from the *mirador* (viewpoint) on the hill as the road winds around to Tarifa, the western end of the Costa del Sol.

EAST TO ALMERÍA

The eastern part of the Costa, from Málaga to Almería, is quieter and less intensively developed. Rincón de la Victoria and Torrox are the first couple of resorts, but you will have to travel to Nerja, the largest resort on this stretch of coast, to find anything approaching those in the western section. Even here, the atmosphere is considerably quieter. Very soon, after the mountains begin to drop precipitously towards the sea, wonderful views can be had from the road, with family resorts like La Herradura and Almuñécar nestled in bays.

This stretch of the Costa del Sol, in the Provincia de Granada, is now known as the Costa Tropical. Motril sits in the middle of an unexpectedly lush green delta, and is guarded to the west by Salobreña and its Moorish castle. Motril to Adra is a conservation area; besides being by far the least built-up of any area on the whole Costa del Sol, it is scenically the most dramatic. Conversely, the route across the plain after leaving Adra is the dreariest along the whole coast. Fortunately, the mountains again meet the sea close to the town of Aguadulce, enlivening the last few kilometres into the city of Almería.

Just east of the city of Almería is the Cabo de Gata natural park, which has some of the most deserted beaches in Andalucía. Heading north from the park, Mojácar is the only resort of any size before the border with Murcia.

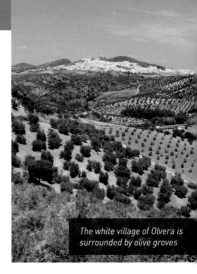

The white village of Olvera is surrounded by olive groves

BEYOND THE COSTA

Visitors who investigate beyond the beaches will find a collection of *pueblos blancos* (whitewashed villages) dotting the landscape of the mountainous interior, and numerous ancient cities whose histories are known throughout the world. There's stunning Sevilla, capital of Andalucía, famed for its bullfights and flamenco, and its wonderful cathedral; Córdoba, the first capital of Moorish Spain; and Granada, capital of the last Moorish kingdom on the Iberian peninsula and home of the magnificent Alhambra palace. This is also where you'll find Jerez de la Frontera, headquarters of the world's sherry trade; Ronda, with its stunning gorge and 18th-century bullring; and Cádiz, considered the oldest city in Spain.

It is these Andalucían towns and cities that come to mind when Spain is mentioned – places that are steeped in history, with romantic palaces, flamenco dancers and a sun-drenched landscape.

A BRIEF HISTORY

Southern Spain is at a geographical crossroads: it is the gateway between the Mediterranean and the Atlantic, and the crossing point between Africa and Europe. The strategic importance of its location has given rise to a long and turbulent history.

The earliest evidence of human occupation is provided by Palaeolithic cave paintings, some 25,000 years old, in the Cueva de la Pileta near Ronda. Neolithic peoples arrived on the scene in the 4th millennium BC, leaving behind signs of early attempts at agriculture and fragments of their pottery. Tribes of Iberians from North Africa crossed over into Spain around 3000 BC and initiated Spain's first experiments in architecture; Spain's oldest structure stands near Antequera, a dolmen burial chamber known as the Cueva de Romeral. After 900 BC, wandering bands of Celts entered the peninsula from northern Europe, bringing their knowledge of bronze and iron work to the area. As they moved further south, the Celts merged with the Iberians and began to build walled villages along the coast.

TRADERS AND COLONISERS

About the same time that this was taking place, the Phoenicians were already venturing across the Mediterranean from their homeland in present-day Lebanon. They reached Spain by about 1100 BC, founding many trading settlements in the land they called *Span* or *Spania*. The first was Gades (modern Cádiz), followed by Malaka (now Málaga) and Abdera (Adra) on the Costa del Sol. Contact with the sophisticated Phoenicians introduced the Celtiberians to the concept of currency.

After 650 BC, Greek traders entered the competition to exploit Spain's rich mineral deposits and fertile land. Their

The Roman Bridge in Córdoba

influence was short-lived, although the olive and the grape, both Greek legacies, soon became important crops.

The Carthaginians, a North African people related to the Phoenicians, subsequently took over much of southern Spain, beginning with Cádiz in 501 BC. They extended their influence along the River Guadalquivir to Sevilla, then to Córdoba. On the coast, they founded the city of Carteya, overlooking the Bay of Algeciras (240 BC). Carthage, challenged by Rome in the First Punic War (264–241), lost most of its Spanish possessions to Iberian attacks. However, its fortunes changed with an initial victory in the Second Punic War (218–201).

Emboldened, the Carthaginian general Hannibal decided to advance on Rome. He led one of history's great military marches from Spain into Italy, crossing the Pyrenees and the Alps on the way. The Romans invaded Spain to cut off Hannibal's supply route – and stayed there for some 600 years.

La Mezquita, a vestige of Moorish Córdoba

ROMAN RULE

It took the Romans two centuries to subdue the Iberians, but in the end most of the peninsula was incorporated into their new colony of Hispania. The south formed part of the province of Baetica, virtually identical to today's Andalucía, with Córdoba its capital.

The Romans had a far-reaching influence on the country. A road network was constructed (the Via Augusta ran the length of the south coast on its way to Rome) and bridges, aqueducts, villas and public buildings were added to the list of their achievements. The introduction of the Latin language (from which modern Spanish developed), Roman law (the basis of Spain's legal system) and, eventually, Christianity, all brought about stability and a degree of unity.

Ultimately the Roman Empire began to crumble and the Romans withdrew from Spain. This left the country to be over-run by various barbarian tribes, especially the Vandals. The

Visigoths, who controlled much of southern Spain for some 300 years, eventually dominated these tribes, but in the end the Visigothic kingdom proved unstable. The monarchy was elective, rather than hereditary, which led to disputes over succession. During one of these altercations, the disaffected party looked to North Africa for an ally.

MOORS AND CHRISTIANS

In AD 711, some 12,000 Berber troops landed at Gibraltar, beginning a period of Moorish rule in Granada and modern Andalucía that was not broken by the Christians until nearly 800 years later. Following their victory at the Battle of Guadalete, the Moors (the name given to the Muslims in Spain) carried all before them. They pushed the Visigoths into the northern mountains and within 10 years most of the Visigothic Kingdom of Hispania had fallen to Islamic rule. They were only stopped from advancing across Western Europe by the West Germanic Franks in 732, at the Battle of Tours in north-central France. Throughout its history, the Moorish Iberian kingdom of Al-Andalus remained in conflict with the Christian kingdoms to the north. However, it remained the dominant force in the Iberian Peninsula for the next 300 years.

The Moors chose Córdoba as their seat of government and from the 8th to the very early 11th century, the city ranked as one of the great cities of the world. It was capital of the independent caliphate

Moorish origins

To this day, Almuñécar, Tarifa, Algeciras, Benalmádena and several other towns are known by their Arabic names. All place names beginning with the prefix Al- have Moorish origins. Almería's Arabic name, for instance, means 'the mirror of the sea'.

of Córdoba, founded by Abd-ar-Rahman III in 929. Under the caliphs, southern Spain knew prosperity and peace, for the Moors were relatively tolerant rulers and taxed non-believers rather than trying to convert them. Intellectual life flourished and great advances were made in science and medicine.

With the introduction of a sophisticated irrigation system, crops such as rice, cotton and sugar cane were cultivated for the first time on Spanish soil, as were oranges, peaches and pomegranates. The manufacture of paper and glass were other Moorish innovations. Skilled engineers and architects, the Moors built numerous palaces and fortifications. As superb craftsmen they excelled in the production of ceramics and tooled leather, as well as delicate silverware.

The ensuing fall of Córdoba was as remarkable as its rise. Christian resistance in northern Iberia gradually solidified during the 8th and 9th centuries with the rise of the kingdoms of Galicia and Asturias, and Charlemagne's efforts to shore up the southern border of the Carolingian Empire, claiming small territories in northern Spain for the Franks. These wins laid the groundwork for the later emergence and expansion of Iberia's other Christian kingdoms from the 9th–14th centuries; Navarre, Léon, Castile, Aragon and Portugal. Spurred on by foreign interests and the hyperbole of the Crusades, these kingdoms were to join the territories of Galicia and Asturias in the Christian 'Reconquista' of Al-Andalus.

In 1009, the caliphate splintered into a number of small kingdoms called *taifas*, which were constantly at war. The Christians in the north, seeing the enemy weakened and divided, captured the *taifa* of Toledo. Under threat of attack, the other *taifas* sought help from the Almoravids, Morocco's Berber dynasty. The Berbers defeated the armies of Alfonso VI, King of León and Castile in 1086. They went on to halt the progress of the

Reconquista and to reduce what was left of Al-Andalus to a province of their own North African Empire.

For a time, the affairs of Muslim Spain were administered from the Almoravid headquarters in Granada, until the Almoravids, softened by a life of ease in Andalucía, lost their grip on the peninsula. The pattern repeated itself a century later when the Moors invoked the aid of the Almohads, from the Atlas

The Alhambra in Granada: the finest memorial to the Nasrids

Mountains of Morocco, in 1151. They soon made themselves the masters of southern Spain and constructed major fortifications, such as Sevilla's Alcázar, endowing the Moors with sufficient strength to resist the Christian forces a while longer.

The fortunes of the Moors and Christians swayed back and forth until 1212, when the Christians gained their first decisive victory at Las Navas de Tolosa in northern Andalucía. The Christians gradually captured and annexed the former bastions of Moorish rule; in 1236, Córdoba fell to Jaime the Conqueror, followed by Sevilla in 1248. The Moors were in retreat, retrenching along the coast and withdrawing to the security of their strongholds in Ronda and Granada.

In military disarray and political decline, Moorish Spain nevertheless saw another two centuries of brilliance under the Nasrid dynasty, founded in Granada by Mohammed I in 1232. Refugees from Córdoba and Sevilla flooded into the city, bringing with them

Sevilla's Giralda: from mosque to bell tower

their talents and skills and adding to the city's brilliance. The magnificent palace of the Alhambra provided the setting for a luxurious court life dedicated to the pursuit of literature, music and the arts.

Yet the Moorish fortresses along the coast soon came under attack. Sancho IV took Gibraltar in 1310, but the Christians later relinquished their prize and the Moors held on to it until 1462. In the 1480s the Christians launched a new offensive; Ronda capitulated to the sovereigns Fernando and Isabel in 1485, followed by Málaga in 1487 and Almería in 1488. Granada was finally conquered in 1492.

THE GOLDEN AGE

With the triumph of Christianity, the country was united under the Catholic Monarchs (*Los Reyes Católicos*), a title conferred by Pope Alexander VI on Fernando II of Aragón and Isabel I of Castilla. Also in 1492, Cristobal Colón (Christopher Columbus) discovered the New World in the name of the Spanish crown. Fanatical in their religious zeal, the king and queen expelled all Jews who refused to convert to Christianity in the same year, followed by the Moors in 1502. The rulers thus reneged on the promise of religious freedom they had given when Granada surrendered. With the Jews who left Spain went many of the country's bankers and merchants, and with the Moors, a good number of its agriculturists and labourers. The converted Jews (*Conversos*) and Moors (*Moriscos*) who remained in Spain were viewed with suspicion by the Inquisition, which had been established by the Catholic Monarchs to suppress heresy. Many fled; many that couldn't were condemned to death.

The 16th century was glorious for Spain, with the conquest of the New World bringing much prestige and wealth. In 1503, the Casa de Contratación in Sevilla was awarded a monopoly on trade with Spain's territories in the Americas. For more than two centuries, Sevilla was the richest city in Spain.

By comparison, coastal settlements languished and were subject to frequent raids by Barbary pirates. Under constant threat for more than 200 years, the population drifted inland, taking refuge in fortified towns and villages hidden in the foothills of the sierras.

Emperor Carlos V of the Holy Roman Empire, the first Habsburg Spanish king, turned his attention to European events. Between 1521 and 1556, he went to war with France four times, squandering the riches of the Americas on endless military campaigns. Carlos also had a weakness for such costly projects as his vast Renaissance palace in the grounds of the Alhambra, which he commissioned in 1526. Taxes imposed on the Moors served to finance the building works, which eventually had to be abandoned for lack of funds when the Moriscos revolted 12 years into the reign of Felipe II (1556–98). The king dispatched his half-brother, Don Juan of Austria, to quell the rebellion, which ended in 1570 with the defeat of the Moriscos and their eventual dispersal. In 1588, Felipe II prepared to invade England, only to be repulsed when the English navy destroyed Spain's previously invincible Armada.

The defeat marked the start of a long decline. Felipe's military forays and his expensive tastes left Spain encumbered with debts. Participation in the Thirty Years' War under Felipe

Ramón Narváez was prime minister several times between 1844–68

III led to further financial difficulties and to another debacle in 1643, when Spanish troops were defeated by the French at Rocroi in Flanders, never to regain their prestige.

FRENCH ASCENDANCY

Spain's internal affairs became the concern of the other great powers after Carlos II died without an heir. The Habsburg Archduke Charles of Austria challenged the French Philip of Bourbon in the ensuing War of the Spanish Succession. Gibraltar was the scene of some fierce fighting in 1704, when Britain captured the Rock on behalf of Austria. Under the terms of the Treaty of Utrecht, which also confirmed Philip's right to the Spanish throne, Spain was finally forced to relinquish its claims to Gibraltar in 1713.

Nearly 100 years later, during the Napoleonic Wars, Spanish ships fought alongside the French fleet against Lord Nelson at Cape Trafalgar (see box). But as the wars continued, Napoleon, distrustful of his ally, forced the Spanish king Fernando VII to abdicate in 1808 and imposed his own brother, Joseph, as king. He then sent thousands of troops across the Pyrenees to subjugate the Spanish, who promptly revolted. Aided by British troops, who were subsequently commanded by the Duke of Wellington, the Spanish drove the French from the Iberian Peninsula. At Tarifa, the enemy was defeated literally overnight in an offensive of 1811. What the English-speaking world knows as the Peninsular War (1808–14) is referred to in Spain as the War of Independence. During this troubled period, Spain's first, short-lived, constitution was drafted and Spanish colonies in South America won their independence.

TROUBLED TIMES

Fernando's return to the throne in 1814 destroyed any hopes left for a constitutional monarchy, but tension between liberals and conservatives led to a century of conflict, marked by the upheavals of the three Carlist wars.

When Fernando died in 1833, his three-year-old daughter María Cristina Isabel was proclaimed queen. Her right to succeed was disputed by supporters of her uncle, Don Carlos, and her succession precipitated the first Carlist war (1833–9).

While Isabel was a child, first her mother then General Baldomero Espartero acted as regents, but in 1843 Espartero was deposed by military officers and Isabel, still only 13, was declared queen in her own right. Her reign, which lasted until

⊘ THE BATTLE OF TRAFALGAR

Fifty kilometres (30 miles) northwest of Tarifa lies the Cabo de Trafalgar (from the Arabic *Tarif al-Gar*, or Cape of the Cave). Off this headland on 21 October 1805, a British fleet of 27 ships under Admiral Horatio Nelson engaged 33 French and Spanish vessels in one of history's most famous naval battles, which established Britain's naval supremacy for the next 100 years. The enemy was routed, losing nearly two-thirds of its ships. No British vessels were lost, but Nelson was hit by a sniper's bullet and died just before the battle's end.

1868, was characterised by political unrest and a series of uprisings. Her government was dominated by military politicians, notably General Ramón María Narváez, Prime Minister several times, and the somewhat more liberal General Leopoldo O'Donnell. Liberal opposition to the regime's authoritarianism became increasingly directed at Isabel. Scandalous reports on the private conduct of the queen, who lived apart from her husband, Francisco de Asís de Borbón, as well as her arbitrary political interference, further damaged the monarchy's cause. An abortive uprising in 1866, and the deaths of O'Donnell and Narváez soon afterwards, weakened her position further. In the autumn of 1868 a successful revolution drove her into exile.

Isabel settled in Paris, where in 1870 she abdicated in favour of her eldest surviving son, Alfonso. After a short-lived First Republic, proclaimed in 1873, Alfonso ascended the throne in 1874 and monarchy returned to Spain for another 50 years.

On the Andalucían coast, the 19th century was a time of tentative expansion. With piracy at an end, a number of towns and villages grew up along the shoreline and the extension of the railway line to Almería in 1899 promoted the early development of the eastern region.

THE SECOND REPUBLIC

Alfonso XIII, just 16 years old, assumed the crown in 1902. Prosperity and stability continued to elude the country, which remained neutral during World War I. Against a murky background of violence, strikes and regional strife, the king accepted the dictatorship of General Miguel Primo de Rivera in 1923. Seven years later, the opposition of radical forces toppled Primo de Rivera from power. King Alfonso went into

exile following anti-roy-
alist election results in
1931 and another repub-
lic was founded.

The parliamentary elec-
tions of 1933 produced
a swing to the right and
public opinion in Spain
became polarised. When
the left came out on top in
the elections of 1936, the
situation began to deterio-
rate at an alarming rate.
Six months later, General
Francisco Franco led a
large section of the army

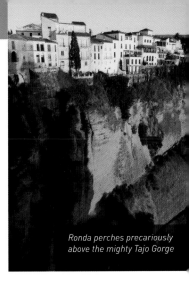

*Ronda perches precariously
above the mighty Tajo Gorge*

against the elected government. Support for the Franco-led
nationalist uprising came from monarchists, conservatives and
the right-wing Falangist organisation, as well as the Roman
Catholic Church, while liberals, socialists, communists and
anarchists sided with the government.

The bloodshed of the Spanish Civil War lasted for three
years and cost hundreds of thousands of lives. Franco
emerged as the leader of a shattered Spain. Many repub-
licans went into exile; others simply disappeared. (The
republican mayor of Mijas caused a sensation when he sur-
faced in the 1960s after three decades in hiding – in his own
home.) Franco kept the impoverished country out of World
War II, despite Hitler's entreaties. The Spanish nation gradually managed to heal its wounds, although conditions were
extremely difficult for many years and life was a struggle for
many people.

CHANGING FORTUNES

All that was to change when Spain's tourist potential began to be exploited in the late 1950s. Spain's admission to the United Nations in 1955, followed by the advent of jet travel and package holidays in the 1960s, subsequently opened up the coast to mass tourism.

With the death of Franco in 1975, Spain became a democracy. The monarchy was restored in the person of King Juan Carlos, the grandson of Alfonso XIII. More than just a figurehead, the king helped to thwart a military coup in 1981, keeping Spain firmly on a democratic course. A process of decentralisation was begun, with powers being devolved to 17 semi-autonomous regions and on 28 February 1982, Andalucía was given autonomous status.

The border with Gibraltar was reopened in February 1985, after a 16-year hiatus, and Spain joined the European Commission in 1986. In 1992 Sevilla hosted Expo '92, and investment poured into Andalucía.

In 2006, several members of Marbella town council were arrested in a corruption scandal based around granting planning permission in return for gifts and favours. And in 2017, two former regional presidents stood trial for fraud and political corruption. The credit crunch of 2008–9 hit Andalucía particularly hard, bringing to an end a building boom that had gone on almost non-stop for forty years and compounding the region's problem of high unemployment, amongst the highest in Spain. Other current political issues include immigration from Eastern European countries, Africa and Latin America and the best way to save what is left of the Costa del Sol's fragile natural environment. After Brexit, Gibraltar has yet again emerged as a highly contentious issue in British–Spanish relations.

HISTORICAL LANDMARKS

c.3000 BC Iberian tribes migrate to Spain from North Africa.

1100 BC Phoenicians found coastal settlements.

900 BC Celts migrate south from northern Europe.

650 BC Greek traders found a series of colonies.

2nd century BC Romans conquer Spain.

5th century AD Visigothic kingdom established.

711 Moors launch their conquest of Spain.

929 Caliphate of Córdoba founded.

1212 Christians defeat Moors at Las Navas de Tolosa.

1232 Nasrid dynasty founded in Granada.

1492 Granada falls to Fernando and Isabel. 'Discovery' of America.

16th century Emperor Carlos V and King Felipe II expand Spain's empire during the Golden Age.

1609 The Moors are finally expelled from Spain.

1704 Great Britain captures Gibraltar.

1808–14 War of Independence against France.

1873 Proclamation of Spain's first (short-lived) republic.

1902–31 Political unrest grows under King Alfonso XIII.

1931–6 Second Republic.

1936–39 Spanish Civil War: at least 600,000 die.

1939–75 Dictatorship of General Francisco Franco.

1975 Spain becomes a constitutional monarchy.

1982 Andalucía is given autonomous status.

1986 Spain enters European Union (then the EC).

1992 Sevilla hosts Expo '92. High-speed train link (the AVE) established.

2002 The euro replaces the peseta as the currency of Spain.

2013 Continuing corruption investigation in Marbella sees 50 people convicted.

2015 Spanish Socialist Workers' Party of Andalusia (PSOE-A) wins regional elections.

2017 Trial of two former regional presidents and 20 other officials accused of political corruption begins in Seville.

The famous cathedral in Sevilla is Europe's third-largest church

WHERE TO GO

Most visitors to Andalucía are based in one of the large coastal resorts on the Costa del Sol to the west of Málaga (Torremolinos, Benalmádena, Fuengirola, Marbella or Estepona), while far fewer head east towards Nerja, Almuñécar, or even as far as Almería. Although the main aim for many is to relax on the beach and soak up as much sun as possible, increasing numbers arrive to play golf. It comes as little surprise, therefore, that the road signs proclaim the area west of Málaga not just as the *Costa del Sol*, but also the *Costa del Golf*.

A growing number of visitors forsake the beach and venture out to the amazingly varied historic towns and cities or to the natural wonders of the national parks buried in this diverse region. Málaga, Ronda, Gibraltar, Sevilla, Córdoba, Granada or the national parks can be visited on a day or overnight trip depending on where you are based.

MÁLAGA

The international airport in **Málaga** ❶ is the gateway to the Costa del Sol and Andalucía for most people. However, few visitors spend much time in the city itself. This is a shame, because Málaga is an ancient Andalucían city of considerable charm that offers a refreshing taste of the real Spain and a diverse selection of interesting museums.

Founded by Phoenician traders more than 3,000 years ago, it came under Carthaginian and Roman rule before falling to the Moorish invasion force in 711. The Moors fortified the city, developing the settlement into a major trading port serving

Granada, and it was one of the last cities in Spain to be reconquered by Christian forces in 1487.

A good place to begin a tour is at Málaga's principal landmark, the **Castillo del Gibralfaro** Ⓐ (from the Arabic *Jebel al Faro* – Lighthouse Hill; daily 9am–6pm, until 9pm in summer). Located some 130 metres (425ft) above the city, this hill is capped by the ramparts of a Phoenician castle reconstructed in the 14th century by the Moors, who went on to build the lighthouse that gave Gibralfaro its name. The walls and parapets, which house an interpretation centre, offer a superb panoramic view of both the city below and the coastline disappearing into the horizon. Because it looks down on the Plaza de Toros, there is also a fine view of the bullring with its small museum.

It is possible to walk up here by taking the stone path and a flight of stairs from the delightful **Paseo del Parque**, with contrasting fountains at either end, which connects the old town with the Plaza de Toros. On its south side, it is a lush seaside tropical garden enhanced by fountains, and behind the Paseo de los Curas, another park, **Palmeral de las Sorpresas**, leads to a pleasant harbour and lighthouse, and to Málaga's outpost of the **Centre Pompidou Málaga** Ⓑ (Wed–Mon 9.30am–8pm; http://centrepompidou-malaga.eu). The small museum exhibits around 70 contemporary works and organises temporary exhibits and events, all well-catered to the younger generation of art-lovers. Nearby, the array of bars and restaurants all

La Manquita

Málaga's vast cathedral is known locally as La Manquita – the one-armed lady – because only one of its twin towers was completed. The north tower soars 100 metres (330ft) above the street, but work on the other, a forlorn stump of stone, stopped in 1783 due to lack of finance.

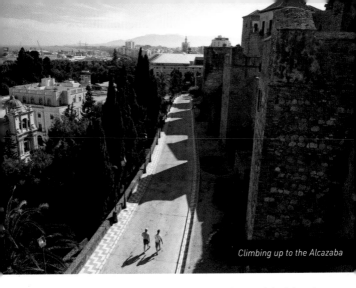

Climbing up to the Alcazaba

benefit from a seaside view extending to the municipal beach **Malagueta**. The other side is home to the smaller Jardínes Puerta Oscura and two impressive buildings, the Ayuntamiento (Town Hall) and the 18th-century La Aduana (Old Custom House), now home to the **Museum of Málaga** (www.museosdeandalucia.es/cultura/museos/MMA, Tue–Sat 9am–8pm, Sun until 3pm, summer Tue–Sun 9am–3pm; free for EU citizens) and its collection of local archaeological finds and fine art.

Immediately behind is the **Alcazaba** Ⓒ (daily 9am–8pm, winter until 6pm), a fortified palace complex built by the Moors in the 8th century. A cobbled path climbs up the hillside within the walls to the Arco del Cristo (Gateway of Christ). The victorious Christian army of Fernando and Isabel celebrated Mass here when the fortress finally fell into their hands in 1487. Beside the entrance to the Alcazaba are the excavated ruins of the 2nd-century **Teatro Romano**, the only visible remains of the Roman city.

Málaga was the birthplace, in 1881, of Pablo Ruiz Picasso, although the artist left his native city at the age of 14 for Madrid and Barcelona. The house where he was born, **Casa Natal Picasso ⓓ** (www.fundacionpicasso.malaga.eu; daily 9.30am–8pm; free Sun after 4pm) at Plaza de la Merced 15, is a small museum and headquarters of the Picasso Foundation. On a much grander scale, the **Museo Picasso ⓔ** (www.museopicasso malaga.org; daily Jul–Aug 10am–8pm, Mar–Jun and Sept–Oct until 7pm, Nov–Feb until 6pm) is housed in the impressive Palacio de Buenavista, which dates from 1542. As well as displaying about 200 of Picasso's works, the museum highlights the city's history and has great temporary exhibitions.

Head north to Plazuela Santísimo Cristo de la Sangre 2 to visit the **Museo del Vidrio y Cristal ⓕ** (www.museovidrioycris-talmalaga.com, Tue–Sun 11am–7pm; guided tours only), which presents the history of the region through the medium of glass and other decorative arts. The beautiful 18th-century building itself is worth a visit.

Head west to Calle Compañía, to the 16th-century Palacio de Villalón, home to the **Museo Carmen Thyssen ⓖ** (www.carmen thyssenmalaga.org; Tue–Sun 10am–8pm; free Sun after 5pm). Its galleries display a remarkable collection of 19th-century Spanish painting focusing on Andalucía; the temporary exhibitions are also excellent.

The **Museo Unicaja de Artes y Costumbres Populares ⓗ** (www.museoartespopulares.com; Mon–Fri 10am–5pm, Sat 10am–3pm, free Tue 1–5pm) on the western edge of the old town offers a fascinating glimpse into how life was lived in Málaga in generations past.

On the way back to the centre of Málaga, stop for a moment or two at the neo-Mudéjar building housing the **Mercado Atarazanas ⓘ** (market; Mon–Sat 8am–2pm). This is also the western boundary of a collection of small roads and pedestrianised streets that end at the main street, Calle Marqués de Larios (now pedestrianised itself), and combine to form Málaga's principal shopping centre. You can buy almost anything here, but remember that the siesta still reigns in this part of Spain and most shops shut at 1 or 2pm and open again at 4 or 5pm.

Further away from the city centre there are three more museums worth a look: the Centro de Arte Contemporáneo de Málaga CAC (http://cacmalaga.eu, Tue–Sun 10am–8pm, summer 10am–2pm, 5–9pm; free) promoting visual arts from the 20th and 21st centuries, the Colección del Museo Ruso (www.coleccionmuseo ruso.es; Tue–Sun 9.30am–8pm), the Spanish branch of the State Russian Museum, and the Museo Automovilistico y de la Moda (www.museoautomovilmalaga.com; Tue–Sun 10am–7pm), where vintage cars and fashion mix in perfect harmony.

WEST OF MÁLAGA

Some of Europe's most popular beach resorts line the coast that stretches 160km (100 miles) to the Rock of Gibraltar.

TORREMOLINOS

Just a few kilometres west of Málaga's international airport lies **Torremolinos ❷**. In the late 1950s and early 1960s, it was the first resort on the

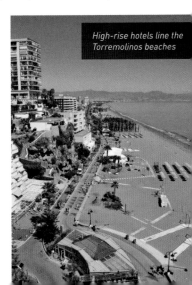

High-rise hotels line the Torremolinos beaches

Costa del Sol to establish a reputation as a popular international playground. Although little more than an overgrown village, it was a haven for young northern Europeans seeking an inexpensive holiday with sun, sand and sangría. Since then, it has built, quite literally, on that reputation, and has long been a highly popular tourist destination, with accommodation for tens of thousands of visitors – much of it in high-rise blocks. Wall-to-wall hotels and apartments reach back in rows from the beaches and there is no denying that it delivers everything sun-hungry visitors could wish for. Miles of glorious beaches, cheap alcohol and familiar food, numerous bars, discos and nightclubs attract a clientele that is largely British, although Germans, Scandinavians and others also arrive in large numbers. This international invasion has completely overwhelmed

⊙ BENALMÁDENA BUDDHISM

High above the Costa del Sol near Benalmádena stands an extraordinarily conspicuous and incongruent religious monument, the **Enlightenment Stupa** (Tue–Sun 10.30am–2pm and 3.30–6.30pm; www.stupabenalmadena.org). Europe's largest stupa (a sacred Buddhist monument) isn't easy to miss when you are driving past on the motorway because of its 33-metre (108ft) golden spire. It's worth visiting for two reasons; the location on a platform high above sea level from which there are expansive views over the coast; and the building itself which inside consists of a light and peaceful prayer hall presided over by a statue of the Buddha. Paintings by Nepalese artists decorate the walls. The whole place radiates a refreshing sense of peace and makes a good place to take a moment out from the pace of life on the beaches below.

Colomares castle in Benalmádena, finished in 1994, is a mix of architectural styles

the town and foreign languages are more dominant than Spanish.

Although the first mention of Torremolinos dates back to 1498, there is really nothing here of historical significance. The town itself, especially **Calle San Miguel**, is simply a profusion of shops. At the bottom of San Miguel a series of winding stairways leads down towards a 7km (4-mile) sweep of golden coastline. This consists of six **beaches** connected by the Paseo Marítimo (beach promenade) and broken only by the rocky promontory of Castillo de Santa Clara, which separates the Bajondillo (east) and Carihuela (west) sections of town.

Chiringuitos (small beachside restaurants) are in plentiful supply, especially in the former fishing village of **La Carihuela**. There are still a few bona-fide fishermen about and if you drag yourself out of bed between 6am and 8am, you'll see them returning in their gaily painted, flat-bottomed wooden boats,

Varied attractions

Selwo has three different enterprises in the area. At Benalmádena, the Selwo Marina (www.selwomarina.es) has dolphin shows and a Penguinarium, while the Selwo Teleférico (http://telefericobenalmadena.com) whisks you up to Monte Calamorro for great views, donkey rides and falconry shows. Further down the coast near Estepona, the Selwo Aventura (www.selwo.es) safari park has some 2,000 animals and also offers African-style accommodation. It is possible to buy a combined pass to all three attractions.

with nets of sardines and anchovies. At lunchtime, you can sample the morning's catch, skewered on a wooden stick and grilled over a fire on the beach.

Many other popular attractions lie nearby, including the wave pools and water slides of **Aqualand** (www.aqualand.es; closed mid-Oct–Apr) and the 18-hole course of the nearby Parador de Málaga Golf. But the biggest draws in Torremolinos are the bars and clubs that have earned the resort its reputation for noisy, non-stop nightlife.

BENALMÁDENA-COSTA

Heading west it appears, at first glance, that Benalmádena-Costa is indistinguishable from its close neighbour, but this isn't really so. It is somewhat less built up and frenetic than Torremolinos, even though it is well endowed with bars, discos and clubs. Its fine beaches stretch for 9km (5 miles), beginning at the large and attractive Puerto Deportivo on the border with Torremolinos. Focal points are the three Moorish watchtowers; the pink, mock-Moorish walls of **Castillo de Bil-Bil**, built by a Frenchwoman in the 1930s and used for concerts, exhibitions and as a tourist office; and one of the Costa del Sol's casinos in the huge and impressive Torrequebrada complex.

Two kilometres (1 mile) inland and high above the sea lies the pretty, whitewashed village of **Benalmádena**. Its **Museo Arqueológico de Benalmádena** (Tue–Sat 10am–1.30pm, 5–7.30pm, Sun 11am–1.30pm) takes pride in its collection of pre-Columbian art, with jewellery, statuary and ceramics from Central America. Also in the Benalmádena area is the **Tívoli World** amusement park (www.tivoli.es), in Arroyo de la Miel (see page 94) and the **Sea Life** aquarium (www.visitsealife. com; daily 10am–6.30pm; last admission an hour before) in Puerto Deportivo.

FUENGIROLA

Located 9km (6 miles) down the road, **Fuengirola** is another resort that's hugely popular with the British. Here bacon and

The rooftops of Mijas

eggs, fish and chips, darts, snooker, English beer and bars showing football matches on television are the norm. But Fuengirola has assimilated this without losing all its Spanish character. This is particularly true in early October, during the annual fair, when the town becomes a blaze of colour and noise and almost every man, woman and child dons typical Andalucían dress.

The Plaza de la Constitución in the town centre has numerous pleasant cafés lining the square beneath the church bell tower, and nearby are the bullring and the Bioparc (zoo; www. bioparcfuengirola.es; daily 10am–6pm, with exceptions at peak times).

Across the river at the western end of town rise the remains of the **Castillo de Sohail** (Wed–Sun 10am–2.30pm). Abd-er-Rahman III built this hilltop fortress in the 10th century and gradually a settlement grew up around the walls. Today its rooms are used for cultural events such as the Fuengirola City Festival and the Medieval and Beer Festivals. Other attractions here include a variety of water sports, a marina, the fishing harbour, a sailing school, the waterslides of the **Mijas Aqua Park** (www. aquamijas.com; closed Oct–Mar), the El Cartujano horse show and horse racing at the Mijas Hippodrome.

A café-lined street in Marbella's old town

MIJAS

Clinging to the hillside 8km (5 miles) inland from Fuengirola is **Mijas ❸**. Surrounded by modern villas and *urbanizaciones* (developments), it looks from the outside like any other quaint village with whitewashed houses. But Mijas is different. Most of the houses have been converted into upmarket shops, restaurants or bars, making the whole village a tourist attraction.

Iglesia de la Encarnación in Marbella

Mijas has a lovely **bullring** and, opposite, beautifully tended gardens slope down to a cliff-top *mirador*, with fine views all along the coast. On one side of this natural balcony you will find a tiny **chapel** dedicated to La Virgen de la Peña, set in a grotto carved from living rock. The Virgin is celebrated in a lively festival in September.

MARBELLA AND PUERTO BANÚS

Sheltered by the mountains of the Sierra Blanca on one side and with the Mediterranean on the other, **Marbella ❹** has earned a reputation for being the most aristocratic of the Costa del Sol's resorts. This began in the 1950s when Prince Alfonso von Hohenlohe bought land and built himself a luxurious home here. It became so popular with his guests that he developed it into the Marbella Club Hotel and that in turn launched Marbella as a trendy gathering place for the jet set in the 1960s. Today the town is still a playground for the rich and famous, frequented by celebrities and politicians, royalty and business tycoons. As a consequence, it has promoted the further development, both here and along the coast, of the largest collection of luxury hotels in Spain.

Marbella is a town in two distinct parts. The largest by far is the modern section and the centre of this, clustered around the palm trees and fountains of the Parque de la Alameda, is taken up with busy pavement cafés, smart boutiques, banks and estate agents' offices. It is at its most attractive, though, by the sea, where the municipality of Marbella encompasses some 28km (17 miles) of beachfront. The promenade winds along the beaches of El Fuerte and Fontanilla, passing Puerto Deportivo, a **marina** with moorings for several hundred pleasure boats, overlooked by the tall spire of the lighthouse. Some lively beach bars and restaurants make this a popular part of town.

The promenade extends west for a mile or two, between attractive apartment complexes and long stretches of golden sands. The monuments of modern Marbella cling to the hills on the western outskirts. The holiday home of the late King Fahd of Saudi Arabia hides behind a row of pines and palms on a hilltop just above the highway, surrounded by high security fences. On a neighbouring hill stands Marbella's modern-style mosque, the **Mezquita del Rey Abdulaziz Al Saud** (open every afternoon 5–7pm except Friday).

But Marbella has its historic side, too. In fact, its

Bonsai collection

Marbella's Museo del Bonsai (daily 10.30am–1.30pm, 4.30–8pm, 3.15–7.30pm in winter) is the only one museum of its kind in Spain and one of the best places on the globe to explore the world of tiny trees.

Glitzy Puerto Banús

history goes back some 1,600 years, even though most of what can be seen, in the town at least, dates from the time of the Catholic Monarchs or later. North of the main road, the **Casco Antiguo** (Old Town) provides an intriguing glimpse of the past, cleverly integrated to cater to modern visitors. First, sit at a café table in the **Plaza de los Naranjos** (Square of the Orange Trees), where you can admire the noble 16th-century façade of the **Ayuntamiento** (Town Hall) and soak up the atmosphere. Then wander through the maze of narrow streets where the white-washed walls are decorated with colourful baskets of flowers.

As you explore the neighbourhood, you'll come across the historic parish church with a landmark bell tower and the convents of La Trinidad and San Francisco (it is said that Miguel de Cervantes, creator of Don Quixote, lodged at the latter). Uphill from the church lie the crumbling walls of the Moorish *castillo*. Scattered throughout this area is an eclectic array of shops and galleries.

Sardines for sale on the beach in Estepona

The **Museo del Grabado Español Contemporáneo** (Museum of Contemporary Spanish Prints; www.mgec.es; Mon and Sat 9am–2pm), housed in the old Bazán Hospital, contains works by Picasso, Miró, Tapiés and other renowned artists.

Along the N-340 national road leading to Puerto Banús, another museum of note is the Museo Ralli (Tues–Sat 10am–3pm; www.rallimuseums.com; free), featuring works by contemporary Latin American and European painters as prestigious as Salvador Dalí, Marc Chagall and Joan Miró.

Just outside Marbella are three other places with ancient historical connections: the **Roman Villa mosaics** dating from the 1st and 2nd centuries at Río Verde near the beach; the Paleo-Christian basilica, **Vega del Mar**, in San Pedro de Alcántara; and **Las Bovedas** (The Cellars), the ruins of Roman baths at Guadalmina.

With the increasing popularity of Marbella, high society has moved west to the chic suburb of Nueva Andalucía and its magnificent harbour, **Puerto Banús**. Sleek, unbelievably expensive yachts line the quayside, and Porsches, Rolls-Royces and Ferrari fill the streets. A glamorous line-up of expensive restaurants and high-class boutiques seem to be permanently open. High rollers haunt the tables in the nearby Casino Marbella, then sip martinis and watch the sun rise from the decks of their luxury yachts. Even if you can't afford to join in, it's fun just to watch how the other half lives.

This part of the Costa del Sol is also a golfer's paradise. There are some 60 golf clubs in operation between Málaga and Sotogrande. These courses cater to all levels, from beginners to professionals. At least half a dozen quality courses can be found between the western edge of Marbella and San Pedro de Alcántara.

OJÉN

Inland from Marbella lie the high peaks of the Sierra Blanca, the most distinctive being La Concha (The Seashell), which rises directly above the town. A scenic road leads to the village of **Ojén** (famous for *aguardiente*, a fierce anise spirit produced here) and on to the mountain pass called Puerto de Ojén. Just beyond, a road on the left leads to the **Refugio de Juanar**, a former hunting lodge, now a hotel, set at the heart of a large national game reserve. The peace and tranquillity found here has attracted numerous personalities, among them General Charles de Gaulle of France, who finished his memoirs here in 1970.

ESTEPONA

The last major resort town on the western part of the Costa del Sol, **Estepona** ❺ provides all the essentials for a good holiday – nice beaches, golf courses, restaurants and a marina – with its old Spanish-town atmosphere retained. Low-rise apartment blocks, simple restaurants and hotels overlook the attractive palm-lined promenade, the **Paseo Marítimo**.

Originally a Roman settlement, Estepona preserves the remains of Moorish fortifications, an 18th-century parish church, a tangle of old narrow streets and an expressionistic bullring. On either side of the town itself, gracious and upmarket hotels are beginning to make an impression on the coastline.

Beyond Estepona, development is more sporadic, although there are some luxury resorts at Sotogrande and Puerto Duquesa. About 6km (4 miles) outside town, a mountain road takes you up to **Casares**, a spectacular white hilltop village clinging precariously to the rugged slopes below its Moorish fort. The road, lined with eucalyptus trees, commands sweeping views of the coast and countryside, and on a clear day the eye is inevitably drawn to the twin peaks known in ancient times as the Pillars of Hercules – the Rock of Gibraltar on the right and Morocco's Jebel Musa on the left.

Gibraltar looms ever larger as you approach **San Roque**, which was established by Spanish refugees who fled the Rock when the English captured it in 1704.. Branch off the main road here and head for **La Línea de la Concepción** and the Rock itself. La Línea experienced a mini-boom when the border with Gibraltar was reopened in 1985 after a blockade lasting 16 years, but it is still a dreary place.

GIBRALTAR

Gibraltar ❻ was a home for pre-historic man: Neanderthal skulls were found in 1848 and 1928 and this is considered one of the final bastions for this species. Although it is known that the Phoenicians, Greeks and Carthaginians were aware of Gibraltar and that the Romans controlled the region from about 500 BC to AD 475, no town was ever built. It wasn't until long after the Moors invaded, in 711, that the first city was constructed. However, even that wasn't completed until nearly 450 years later, in 1160.

The next three centuries saw numerous battles and it was not until 1462 that the Spanish finally reconquered Gibraltar. In

The Rock of Gibraltar, once thought to be the edge of the world

the early 18th century, problems over succession to the Spanish throne led to an Anglo-Dutch force capturing Gibraltar in 1704. Under the Treaty of Utrecht in 1713 Spain ceded its rights to Gibraltar to the British – although not without a fight. In 1727, their first siege failed, as did the Great Siege (1779–83), when Spanish and French forces totalling 50,000 men attacked just 5,000 defenders. Despite nearly four years of hardship, the British refused to surrender. In 1830 Gibraltar achieved the status of a British Crown Colony, which it still holds.

The town and harbour lie on the east slope of the Rock, overlooking the bay, with the narrow defile of **Main Street** cutting through the middle. This is lined with duty-free shops selling alcohol, perfume, cameras and electronic goods, and English-style pubs serving pints of bitter. The currency is the Gibraltarian pound (equal to the British pound), but shops and other businesses accept both sterling and euros.

Also at sea level is the **Gibraltar Museum** (www.gibmuseum. gi; Mon–Fri 10am–6pm, Sat 10am–2pm), with what are considered to be the best-preserved Moorish baths in Europe. The museum has interesting exhibits on Gibraltar's history. Of interest, too, is **Nelson's Anchorage**, where Admiral Nelson's body is said to have been brought in a barrel of rum after the Battle of Trafalgar in October 1805. Nearby is a 100-tonne Victorian super-gun, the largest of its type in the world.

Main Street ends at the Referendum Gates, and beyond lies the **cable-car station** (daily 9.30am–7.15pm), where you can take a trip to the top of the Rock, with a stop halfway to visit the **Apes' Den**. The so-called Barbary apes (actually tailless macaque monkeys) that inhabit the Rock are natives of North Africa, descended from animals brought over by sailors as pets and ships' mascots. Legend has it that if the apes ever leave the Rock, then British rule will come to an end. When the apes' population declined significantly during World War II, Winston Churchill was worried and the primates have been well cared for ever since. The views from the summit 426 metres (1,400ft) up are spectacular, particularly across the strait to Morocco, along the coast towards Estepona and down the sheer east face of the Rock to the water-holding areas (for desalination) and the beaches of Sandy Bay, Catalan Bay and Eastern Beach.

From the upper cable car station you can follow the paths around the **Upper Rock Nature Reserve** (daily 9.30am–6.15pm, until 7.15 in summer), which has a dense Mediterranean scrub vegetation harbouring 530 kinds of plant, including some rare species, growing on the alkaline limestone soils. This area is good for birdwatching too, especially during the spring and summer migrations when Gibraltar marks the shortest route between Europe and Africa.

St Michael's Cave is an impressive natural grotto containing stalagmites and stalactites, which is sometimes used as a venue for musical performances. At the north end of the Rock are the **Great Siege Tunnels**, a system of galleries blasted through the inside of the rock face during the 18th-century Great Siege. The tunnels excavated during World War II can be visited by prior booking (tel: +350 2007 1649). It was from these that General Eisenhower conducted the Allied invasion of North Africa.

Picturesque alleyway in Tarifa

ALGECIRAS

Just across the bay from Gibraltar is an uninspiring port town whose only saving grace, on good days at least, is its unsurpassed views of the Rock. From the harbour, hydrofoils and car ferries cross the strait to Ceuta, a Spanish protectorate in North Africa, and to Tangier in Morocco. A day trip to Ceuta is certainly possible, but there is not much of interest there, beyond shopping.

TARIFA

Tarifa ❼ is where the waters of the Mediterranean mingle with those of the Atlantic and bring the Costa del Sol to an end. Europe looks across the Strait of Gibraltar to Africa, with the Rif Mountains of Morocco dominating the horizon a mere 13km

(8 miles) away. A section of the old Moorish walls remain, as does the 10th-century fortress.

However, it is not its history that attracts most visitors these days. The beaches stretching to the west are such a mecca for windsurfers and kitesurfers that Tarifa is often called the windsurf capital of Europe. The prevailing wind, known as the *poniente*, is from the west, making the beaches among the windiest in Europe.

The windsurfers are not the only ones to take advantage of the reliable breeze; the hillsides above the town have sprouted a forest of wind-powered electricity turbines. In spring and autumn, storks, buzzards and other soaring birds fill the skies as they climb in the rising thermals before gliding across the strait on their annual migration, congregating here where the sea crossing is at its shortest.

EAST OF MÁLAGA

The eastern part of the Costa del Sol stretches for over 200km (125 miles) from Málaga all the way to Almería. This part of the coast has a very different feel from the western section, with less intensive development and, in parts, a much rockier and more attractive shoreline.

MÁLAGA TO NERJA

Leaving Málaga's suburbs, you arrive immediately in **Rincón de la Victoria**, a resort given over to weekend apartments owned by Spanish city-dwellers. Prehistoric man was here first, occupying the **Cueva del Tesoro** (Treasure Cave; daily summer 10.30am–1pm and 4.30–7pm, winter until 5pm) on the Málaga side of the town. Cave paintings and prehistoric remains have been discovered, and there is a beautiful underground lake with

Tarifa's beaches stretching away to the west

stalactites. According to legend, five Moorish kings buried some huge treasure inside the cave, but it has never been found.

Torre del Mar is the gateway to the wine region of the Axarquía, and its capital, **Vélez-Málaga**, which lies 4km (2.48 miles) inland. Founded by the Phoenicians, Vélez sprawls around an historic centre dominated by a Moorish *alcazaba* (citadel) and two venerable churches: the late-Gothic Iglesia de San Juan Bautista and the Iglesia de Santa María.

NERJA

Nerja ❽ is the one large international resort to the east of Málaga and it's a popular destination for British, German and Scandinavian visitors. The nightlife is lively, though quieter than in Torremolinos, and the beaches, which are tucked into rocky coves, are prettier, if somewhat smaller. The area also offers good opportunities for hiking, horse-riding, scuba diving, snorkelling and angling, giving Nerja the edge for those seeking an active holiday.

The only sight to see in town is the **Balcón de Europa**, a palm-fringed cliff-top promenade jutting out over the sea, dividing the sandy crescent of La Caletilla beach on the west from La Calahonda on the east.

Just 6km (4 miles) east of the beach of **Maro** is the famous **Cueva de Nerja** (Cave of Nerja; www.cuevadenerja.es; daily 9am–3pm, Jul–Aug Thu–Fri until 5.30pm). This huge cavern was discovered in 1959 when a group of local boys stumbled on it one day while they were out hunting bats. Floodlights illuminate the impressive limestone formations, which include a stalagmite/stalactite over 32 metres (105ft) high and 18 metres (59ft) in diameter. Archaeological remains confirm that these caves were inhabited 30,000 years ago. The Nerja Festival of Music and Dance, held in July, takes place in the Sala de la Cascada, which has wonderful acoustics.

⊘ TROPICAL FRUIT

The coast of Granada province provides a perfect microclimate for the cultivation of exotic crops. Until not long ago, there was a thriving sugar refining industry here. You can still buy bottles of locally distilled rum and there are stands of sugar cane on the coastal plain here but most of the sugar milling machines now adorn roundabouts in Salobreña and Motril (where there is a museum to the vanished industry). Nowadays, the farmers of the 'Costa Tropical' specialise in sub-tropical fruits for the table, especially avocados, mangoes and custard apples (*chirimoyas*). You'll find all these on sale in shops, markets and at roadside stalls in season.

Inland from Nerja, the corrugated hills of the Sierra de Tejeda rise up toward the village of **Frigiliana**. Under the Moors, it was one of the many prosperous villages within the Kingdom of Granada. Today, the historic centre is regarded as an outstanding example of Moorish village architecture, with a lovely 16th-century church and ruined Moorish castle.

The coast at Nerja

COSTA TROPICAL

After Nerja, the scenery changes dramatically; the mountains begin to cascade to the sea and the panoramas of the ragged coastline are magnificent. Just before La Herradura, a neat little town with a nice beach, road signs proclaim that you are now in the Provincia de Granada. Until you pass into Almería, this part of the Costa del Sol, the most attractive but least known, is officially called the Costa Tropical.

Almuñécar is the first town of any size and has an ancient history. A fine **aqueduct** stands as a monument to the skills of the Roman engineers who constructed it during the reign of Antoninus Pius in the 2nd century AD. A port for Granada in Moorish times, Almuñécar continued to enjoy a certain prestige after the Reconquest, when Juan de Herrera, the architect of El Escorial, Philip II's grand monastery-cum-palace near Madrid, was commissioned to design the parish church.

Almuñécar's best-known attraction is the **Castillo San Miguel** (Tue–Sat 10am–1.30pm and 4–6.30pm, Sun 10am–1pm), dating from the 8th through to the 15th century and standing on the hill on which the Old Quarter is built.

These days the town, set around an attractive curving beach, is an increasingly popular family resort. Attractions include the **Parque Ornitológico Loro Sexi** (Tue–Sat Jan–Mar and Oct–Dec 10.30am–2pm and 4–6pm, Apr–May, Jun and Sept 10.30am–2pm and 5–8pm, Jul–Aug until 9pm; http://parquelorosexi.almunecar.es), on the slopes below the castle, and a waterpark (https://aqua-tropic.com) on the seafront.

Along the road from Almuñécar, pretty villas with spectacular coastal views dot the hillsides until, all of a sudden, the scenery changes dramatically. As the coast flattens out, a town of white-washed houses clinging to the slopes of a rocky, cone-shaped hill comes into view. **Salobreña** is an impressive sight. A Moorish castle, beautifully restored, stands at the top of the town.

Salobreña stands as the gateway to the agriculturally rich *vega* (plain) of the thriving port city of **Motril ⑨**. Sugar cane, the source of the greenery, used to flourish here. The sugar refineries in the area once earned the town its nickname – Little Cuba. Like Cuba, Motril is known for its rum. Motril's proximity to the Alpujarra and Sierra Nevada mountains has increased tourism here substantially. Weekly cruise ships now dock at the port, and to cater to these transient visitors golf courses, shopping centres, parks, museums, hotels, recreational facilities, and new access roads have opened up. Motril and Salobreña have their own extensive beaches and there are many more to come as the road continues eastward.

The next 40km (25 miles) is a conservation area and the least developed of any section of the coast. The small towns and villages, reminiscent of what the rest of the Costa used to be like before the tourist invasion, have only a few hotels, which means that even in midsummer, the beaches are far from overcrowded. What's more, it's possible to be swimming in the Mediterranean while the snow-covered peaks of the Sierra Nevada shimmer in the distance.

Salobreña detail

This scenery changes, and much for the worse, after **Adra**. The N340/E15 crosses a vast and dreary plain before it rejoins the coast at **Aguadulce**. Here, the mountains meet the sea again and the journey on to Almería is short but attractive.

ALMERÍA

Rich in history, **Almería ⑩** was once the most important city in Moorish Spain. The Almería of today is a pleasant, provincial capital that's worth a visit if your travels take you to the eastern limits of the Costa del Sol.

There are two major sights. One is Abd-er-Rahman III's massive **Alcazaba** (Apr–Oct Tue–Sun 9am–8.30pm, Nov–Mar Tue–Sun 9am–6.30pm; free admission for EU citizens), which looms large on the hilltop above the city. Although an earthquake caused extensive damage in 1522, the crenellated ochre walls and a section of the turreted ramparts stood firm, and now provide wide-ranging vistas over the city and the sea. The second is the forbidding, fortified **Catedral** (Cathedral;

Mon–Fri 10am–2pm, 4–6pm; charge) that stands just inland from the waterfront Paseo de Almería. It was built in the 16th century, when Barbary pirates were terrorising the coast. The Museo de Almería (mid-Sept–mid-Jun Tue–Sat 9am–8pm, Sun 9am–3pm; rest of the year Tue–Sun 9am–3pm and Wed–Sat 6–9.30pm) displays archaeological finds dating from 3000 BC to the demise of Arab rule in Andalucía.

Inland from Almería lies one of the most un-European landscapes on the European continent. The **Sierra de Alhamilla** is a desert of barren mountains, rocky ravines and dry gravel riverbeds; spiky agave plants and prickly pears are the only vegetation. The region's uncanny resemblance to the American West made it a popular film location for spaghetti westerns, including such classics as *A Fistful of Dollars* and *The Good, the Bad and the Ugly*. Near the village of Tabernas is an area known as **Mini-Hollywood**, where three of the film sets have been preserved as independent tourist attractions. Oasys Park (daily 10am–7pm, until 9pm Jul–Aug, weekends only in winter; www.oasysparquetematico.com), incorporates a zoological reserve featuring many species of Iberian and African creatures, including lions, reptiles and birds, and an aquatic zone with pools, slides for children and jacuzzi for adults.

ACROSS THE MOUNTAINS TO CÁDIZ

For a complete contrast to the sun, sea and sangría atmosphere of the coast, Antequera, Ronda and other 'White Towns' are easily reached from the busiest part of the Costa del Sol. Or you can cross the mountains to Jerez de la Frontera and Cádiz, with their access to the superlative Doñana National Park. The great inland cities of Andalucía are covered in the next section (see page 64).

Limestone formations of El Torcal

ANTEQUERA AND EL TORCAL

Set in a rich, fertile plain 47km (29 miles) north of Málaga, the market town of **Antequera ⑪**, which has been inhabited since prehistoric times, has a cluster of monuments uphill from the tourist information office. Through the 16th-century 'Giants' Arch' gateway (Arco de los Gigantes) is a Renaissance church, the **Real Colegiata de Santa María la Mayor** (Wed–Mon 10am–6pm, Tue 2–6pm; free). Beside it is the entrance to the ruined Muslim castle of the Alcazaba (Wed–Mon 10am–6pm, Tue 2–6pm; free). On the outskirts of town are three enormous **prehistoric burial chambers**: the Dólmen de Menga, probably constructed around 2500 BC, the Dolmen de Viera and the Dólmen del Romeral.

South of Antequera is a well-known beauty spot, the karst limestone formations of **El Torcal de Antequera**. The rocks here were laid down in the Jurassic period 150 million years ago and have since been shaped into abstract forms by the movement of

The vertiginous Tajo Gorge cuts through the town of Ronda

the earth and by wind erosion. From the car park and information centre in the middle of El Torcal (information centre: daily 10am–5pm, until 7pm in summer; www.torcaldeantequera.com), follow the 'green' walking route, which takes about an hour to complete and takes in the viewpoint of **Las Ventanillas**, from which you can even see the North African coast on a clear day.

RONDA

The opening of an improved road from San Pedro de Alcántara to **Ronda** ⓬ has ended the isolation of this mountain area and shortened the driving time from the coast to an hour. One of the most spectacularly situated towns in Europe, Ronda sits atop a cliff-bound plateau, cleaved through the middle by a sheer-sided gorge. The older, Moorish part of town (La Ciudad) lies to the south of the ravine, linked by an 18th-century bridge to El Mercadillo, the more modern district that arose after the Christian Reconquest.

The gorge, known as **El Tajo**, is a deep and narrow crevasse that plunges 150 metres (490ft) to the foaming Río Guadalevín, a tributary of the Guadiaro. You can enjoy a superb view of the Tajo and the patchwork of fields beyond from the **Puente Nuevo** (New Bridge; interpretation centre: Mon–Fri 10am–6pm, Sat–Sun 10am–3pm), built in 1788, and from the walkways that follow the edge of the gorge.

To see some of Ronda's most important monuments, cross the bridge into **La Ciudad**, the old Moorish enclave that remained impervious to Christian assault until 1485. On one side of the Plaza de Campillo square stands the **Palacio de Mondragón** (Mon–Fri 10am–6pm, Sat, Sun and hols 10am–3pm; until 7pm in summer), constructed by Abomelic, King of Ronda, in 1314 and later taken over by the Christian conquerors. A distinguished Renaissance portal, a later addition, opens onto spacious court-yards where horseshoe arches and distinctive tile ornaments indicate the Moorish origins of this grand building. The palace now houses the **Museo Municipal** (Municipal Museum) where you can learn about the history of the town and the surrounding area.

Just a short distance away, Ronda's original mosque survives in the form of the **Iglesia de Santa María la Mayor** (Mon–Sat 10am–6pm, Sun 10am–12.30pm and 2–6pm). The minaret was converted into a bell tower and a Gothic nave was tacked on to the original structure, followed by a high altar in ornate 16th-century Plateresque style and some finely carved Baroque choir stalls. The church overlooks the Plaza de la Duquesa de Parcent, the main square, with the long, elegant facade of the **Ayuntamiento** (Town Hall) gracing another side. The nearby Palacio de Moctezuma houses the **Museo Unicaja Joaquín Peinado** (Mon–Fri 10am–5pm, Sat 10am–3pm; www.museojoaquinpeinado.com) dedicated to the 20th-century painter from Ronda.

Heading back towards the Puente Nuevo, stop to view the exterior of the **Palacio del Marqués de Salvatierra**, an 18th-century mansion

Unspeakable end

During the Spanish Civil War, Nationalist sympathisers in Ronda were hurled to their deaths in the gorge, an event recalled by Ernest Hemingway in his novel *For Whom the Bell Tolls*.

famous for its wrought-iron balconies. Nearby stands **La Mina y Jardines de Forestier – Casa del Rey Moro** (The Mine and Forestier Gardens – Moorish King's House; gardens only open to the public daily 10am–6pm), where you will find the remnants of a 14th-century water mine, and gardens designed by the French landscaper Jean Claude Nicolas Forestier in the 1920s. A flight of over 300 steps cut out of the rock in Moorish times leads down from the garden to a spring in the gorge.

Beyond here, the road curves down towards the Tajo, where two more bridges – the **Puente Viejo** (Old Bridge), built on Roman foundations, and the Moorish **Puente Arabe** – span the gorge and offer striking views of the chasm. Down by the river stand the **Baños Árabes** (Moorish Baths; Mon–Fri 10am–6pm, Sat, Sun and hols 10am–3pm), their vaulted roof still intact.

Immediately back across the Puente Nuevo, a *parador* (see page 113) occupies what was the old Town Hall and just beyond that is Ronda's famous **Plaza de Toros y Museo Taurino** (Bullring and Bullfighting Museum; www.rmcr.org; Apr–Sept 10am–8pm, Mar and Oct 10am–7pm, Nov–Feb 10am–6pm). Ronda is regarded as the cradle of modern bullfighting, and the bullring is the oldest in Spain, known for its monumental colonnade protecting the double-tiered seating.

THE WHITE TOWNS

If one archetypal image of Andalucía is its endless sandy beaches, another is the ubiquitous whitewashed mountain town, a labyrinth of narrow, stepped and winding streets clinging to the hillside or edging up to a crag or cliff. The most attractive white towns and villages are scattered over the mountains between Ronda and the east coast.

One of the most accessible is **Grazalema**, which serves as a service centre for visitors to the nature reserve of the same

The beautiful white town of Olvera

name. The slopes around Grazalema support forests of the rare Spanish fir, *abies pinsapo*, watered by the highest rate of rainfall in Spain. Across the hills is the handsome white town of **Arcos de la Frontera** – its name hinting at the times when such places stood on the border between Muslim and Christian dominions. Other white towns worth linking up in a tour starting out from Ronda are **Setenil de las Bodegas**, **Olvera** and **Zahara de la Sierra**.

CÁDIZ

The ancient city of **Cádiz ⑬**, sitting at the end of a very narrow peninsula of land that runs parallel to the coast, was founded by the Phoenicians in 1100 BC and is considered to be Spain's oldest town. In fact, Cádiz's amazing amalgam of history is not readily apparent, with only the remains of the old Roman theatre betraying the city's age. It was conquered by Alfonso X in 1262 and granted the monopoly of trade with Africa by

The Catedral, Cádiz

the Catholic Monarchs in 1493. Columbus also departed from this city on his second and fourth voyages in 1493 and 1502 respectively. In the latter part of the 16th century, it twice came under attack from enemy naval forces and a period of prosperity ensued when the Casa de Contratación, the monopoly rights for trade with the Americas, was transferred from Sevilla by order of Felipe V in 1717. A century later, on 19 March 1812, while under attack from Napoleon's forces, the national parliament met in the church of San Felipe Neri and proclaimed the first Spanish parliament.

The town has some fascinating cultural attractions but of most interest is the architecturally contrasting Baroque and classical **Catedral** (Mon–Sat 10am–6.30pm, Sun 1.30–6.30pm), which was constructed between 1772 and 1838. The elegant **Hospital de Mujeres** (Women's Hospital; Mon–Fri 10am–1.30pm and 5.30–8pm, Sat 10am–1.30pm), built even earlier, in 1749, is notable for its patio and art collection, including a fine El Greco. The ceiling of the unusual **Oratorio de la Santa Cueva** church is adorned by five spectacular paintings – three of which are fine examples of Goya's work. The church of **San Felipe Neri**, mentioned above, is also well worth a look. Another highlight is **Torre Tavira** (Tavira Tower, daily 10am–6pm, until 8pm in summer; www.torretavira.com), one of 129 watchtowers and the highest point in the old town, which offers amazing views of the city and a Camera Obscura experience. Gourmets should also pay a visit to the wonderful **Mercado Central** (Mon–Sat 9am–3pm; food court also Tue–Sat 8pm–midnight) with dozens of stands offering fresh produce and a food court where you can try local delicacies.

EL PUERTO DE SANTA MARÍA

This small town, on the coast of the Bay of Cádiz, looks across to Cádiz and has considerable charm. Foreign visitors are only just starting to discover this area, but the Spanish flock here in their thousands, especially in August when there are a series of bull-fights. At that time, the seafood restaurants, for which El Puerto is famous, are full until the early hours. Apart from the endless wineries, fine beaches and water sports, there isn't too much to do here, but El Puerto de Santa María is one of those places to be savoured for its atmosphere. Located between Jerez de la Frontera and Cádiz, El Puerto is easily reached by road or rail. However, the nicest way to get here is on the small ferry that plies its way between Cádiz and the dockside in El Puerto.

JEREZ DE LA FRONTERA

The name **Jerez de la Frontera** ⑭ is indicative of two things. It once lay close to the frontier of the old Moorish kingdom of Granada, hence de la *Frontera*. And *Jerez* (pronounced khe-*reth*) gave its name to the wine that has made the town famous, better known to the world as sherry.

Although known as long ago as the Phoenician era,

Bodega tours

Most *bodegas* in Jerez organise guided tours, generally only on weekdays. The visits include a full explanation of the cultivation methods and the production process.

Jerez first came to prominence under the Moors in the 11th–12th century, and it is from that period that the impressively walled and towered **Alcázar** dates. Inside is a simple but elegant mosque that was later converted into a chapel dedicated to Santa María la Real. Reconquered by King Alfonso X in 1264, it became one of the most prosperous towns in Andalucía after the discovery of the Americas and the unification of Spain in 1492. Below the Alcázar is the **Colegiata** (Collegiate Church), a dark stone building dating from the 17th century. Housed within is the image of *Cristo de la Viña* (Christ of the Vineyard).

It was the development of the sherry and brandy business that brought the city worldwide acclaim and more prosperity. It is impossible to miss the *bodegas* of such prestigious old firms as Harveys, Williams & Humbert, Gonzalez-Byass and Pedro Domecq. As some of the names imply, it was a group of English merchants who launched Jerez as the world capital of fortified wine. Three centuries on, their descendants still control the sherry trade.

Jerez is also famous for its horses. The aristocracy built vast ranches alongside its vineyards. The Domecq family established the **Real Escuela Andaluza del Arte Ecuestre** (Spanish Riding School; see websites for

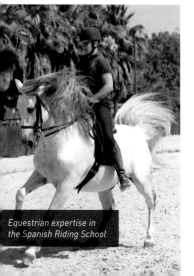

Equestrian expertise in the Spanish Riding School

tour times, www.realescuela.org) in 1973 as a showcase for Andalucían equestrian skills. Dressage exhibitions are held on specific dates (check schedule online), but visitors can watch practice sessions on other mornings. Entrance fee includes El Museo del Enganche (Horse Carriage Museum) and Museo del Arte Ecuestre (Museum of Equestrian Art).

Jerez has other attractions, too. In addition to churches and mansions, there's the **Centro Andaluz de Flamenco** (Mon–Fri 9am–2pm; www.centroandaluzdeflamenco.es; free) in the Palacio Pemartín and the Zoo Botánico (www.zoobotanicojerez.com; Tue–Sun May–Sept 10am–7pm, Oct–Apr until 6pm).

PARQUE NACIONAL DE DOÑANA

Listed as a World Heritage Site, the **Parque Nacional de Doñana** ⑮ is probably the most famous park in Spain, with a host of national and international awards to its name. Covering 862 sq km (333 sq miles), it is bordered on one side by the Atlantic Ocean and on another by the Río Guadalquivir, as it winds down from Sevilla to reach the ocean at Sanlúcar de Barrameda.

The Doñana is the last great lowland wilderness sanctuary in southern Europe and has three distinct ecosystems: the *marismas* (salt marshes), the *matorral* (brushwood) and the *dunas* (sand dunes). Within its bounds can be found an amazing array of wildlife, but birds are the main attraction. More than 350 species have been recorded here – and you might have an opportunity to see 170 species in the summer and 220 in winter. The most popular way to get a general perspective of the Doñana is on a tour organised by Cooperativa Andaluza Marismas del Rocío (www.donanavisitas.es), whose large-wheeled buses depart from the visitors' centre at **El Acebuche**.

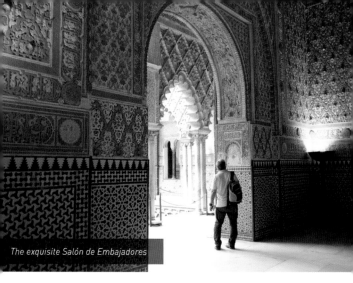

The exquisite Salón de Embajadores

GREAT CITIES OF ANDALUCÍA

No trip to Andalucía would be complete without seeing at least one of its great inland cities. Sevilla, Córdoba and Granada are repositories of an incredibly rich heritage. The smaller cities of Baeza and Úbeda are also well worth a visit.

SEVILLA

The capital of Andalucía, **Sevilla** ⑯ is the most Spanish of Spanish cities. It is also one of the most beautiful cities in the world, exuding a sensual, spiritual and romantic atmosphere. It was already a thriving riverside settlement when Julius Caesar arrived in 45 BC and under the Romans it developed into a major town. Subsequently, Sevilla became the capital of the Visigothic kingdom and then of a Moorish *taifa*, before falling to Fernando III in 1248. A monopoly of trade with the New World brought the city to its peak during the Golden Age. 'Madrid is the capital of Spain,' the saying went, 'but Sevilla is the capital of the world.'

Sevilla is full of historic buildings and museums but the two most prominent monuments in the city are around the Plaza del Triunfo. Work on the **Catedral** and **La Giralda** Ⓐ (Mon 11am–3.30pm, Tue–Sat 11am–5pm, until 4pm Jul–Aug, Sun 2.30–6pm, free Mon from 4.30pm) began in 1401 after the great mosque was razed. The new building followed the ground plan of the old mosque, hence its unusually broad, rectangular form. It is the third-largest Christian church in Europe after St Peter's in Rome and St Paul's in London.

Massive without, and richly decorated within, the cathedral contains over 30 chapels, including the central **Capilla Mayor** with its Flemish altarpiece and the **Capilla Real** (Royal Chapel), the last resting place of Fernando III, the 'King-Saint' who delivered Sevilla from the hands of the infidel. The silver-gilt key to the city, presented to Fernando by the vanquished Moors, can be seen in the treasury.

On the north side of the cathedral lies the **Patio de los Naranjos** (Court of the Orange Trees), the ceremonial court-yard of the old mosque with its original ablutions fountains. The minaret, dating from 1184, was preserved as the bell tower of the cathedral. This celebrated tower, **La Giralda** (same hours as the Cathedral), is Sevilla's most famous landmark. The exterior is beautifully decorated with typical *sebka* brickwork, which contrasts vividly with the bland interior, where a series of 35 gently elevating ramps lead to an observation platform at a height of 70 metres (230ft) above the

Horseplay

To celebrate the recapture of Sevilla by the Christians in 1248, Fernando III of Castile rode his horse to the top of the Giralda.

ground. This is the finest *mirador* in Sevilla and provides stunning views of the old city below. It is surprising to note just how large the Plaza de Toros is when seen from this angle. Look up and you will see how the tower came by its name. In 1356 an earthquake destroyed the original ornamental top and it wasn't until 1558 that the height was raised to 98m (322ft) by the addition of the huge bells and a weathervane (*giralda* in Spanish) in the form of a statue of a beautiful goddess representing Faith.

The **Real Alcázar** Ⓑ (www.alcazarsevilla.org; daily 9.30am–5pm, Apr–Sept until 7pm; free on Mon Apr–Sept 6–7pm and Oct–Mar 4–5pm) is a major monument to mid-14th-century Mudéjar architecture, combining Moorish, Gothic and Renaissance elements. Built by Moorish craftsmen under Christian rule, during the reign of Pedro the Cruel, the rambling palace and its several courtyards incorporate fragments of an earlier Moorish fortress

---

⊙ SEVILLA'S APRIL FAIR

Sevilla has two big annual celebrations, both in spring. The first, Semana Santa (Holy Week), is Easter Week, a mixture of religious solemnity and exuberant ostentation. Straight after it comes the hedonistic April Fair (*Feria de Abril*), which is best thought of as a week-long party extolling all things Andaluz: song and dance, food and drink, horses and bulls. For the duration of the Fair, life in Sevilla moves across the river from the city centre to a purpose-built fairground. During the day finely dressed men and women parade around in horses and horse-drawn carriages. By evening, after the afternoon's bullfight in the Maestranza bullring, the fairground starts to fill up with people there to dance to the sound of flamenco rhythms and to drink glasses of chilled fino sherry.

and blend Christian motifs with Moorish designs. The most interesting part is the Patio de las Doncellas (Courtyard of the Maidens), where the rooms preserve outstanding decorative features – ornamental tiles, carved stucco and characteristic coffered ceilings. Fans of the *Game of Thrones* TV series will recognise the Alcázar as the Palace of the Kingdom of Dorne, just as *Star Wars* aficionados will identify the Plaza de España as the Palace of the Kingdom of Naboo.

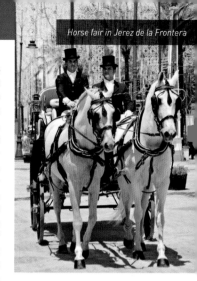
Horse fair in Jerez de la Frontera

The ornate, domed **Salón de Embajadores** (Hall of the Ambassadors) is equal to anything in the Alhambra. Next door is the glass-roofed Patio de las Muñecas (Courtyard of the Dolls), so named for the two tiny human faces carved into the decoration surrounding one of the Moorish arches. These are most unusual, as Muslim craftsmen were forbidden by their religion to depict the human form in their art.

Returning to the entrance courtyard, take the narrow passage on the right to the Patio de María Padilla, which sits on top of underground baths. The apartments beyond are hung with Flemish tapestries recording Carlos V's Tunis Expedition of 1535, one of them showing an upside-down map of the Mediterranean. Not to be missed, either, are the beautiful Gardens, an oasis of tranquillity in this perpetually busy city.

Nestled around the walls of the Alcázar is the **Barrio de**

Santa Cruz, the old Jewish quarter, a picturesque maze of narrow lanes with whitewashed houses and tiny shaded patios that invite leisurely exploration. Just south of the cathedral stands the former exchange building, Casa Lonja, which is now the **Archivo de Indias** (Mon–Sat 9.30am–5pm, Sun 10am–2pm; free) with a valuable collection of documents relating to the discovery and conquest of the Americas.

Nearby, on the banks of the river, is another of Sevilla's icons. The **Torre del Oro** Ⓒ (Gold Tower; Mon–Fri 9am–6.45pm, Sat–Sun 10.30am–6.45pm; charge) is all that remains of Sevilla's medieval fortifications and in times of possible invasion a huge metal chain was stretched between here and the other riverbank to protect the harbour. Originally used to store treasures brought from the Americas, it is now home to the small **Museo Marítimo** (Maritime Museum). Just north of here, another of the city's landmarks is the **Plaza de Toros** with its **Museo Taurino, Real Maestranza de Caballería** Ⓓ (Bullring and Bullfighting Museum; www.realmaestranza.com; daily 9.30am–7pm, later in summer, until 3pm on days of bullfights; charge).

Further north again, a visit to the **Museo de Bellas Artes** Ⓔ (Museum of Fine Arts; Jan–mid-Jun and mid-Sept–Dec Tue–Sat 9am–8pm, Sun 9am–3pm, mid-Jun–mid-Sept Tue–Sun 9am–5pm) will remind visitors that Sevilla is the birthplace of two of Spain's greatest artists, Velázquez and Murillo.

Seville has some spectacular modern architecture, too, such as the iconic

Favoured status

Carmona's history is unusual because the town was never under feudal rule, but was protected as a satellite of the crown. That is why it is endowed with such an extraordinary number of palaces, mansions, convents and churches.

Metropol Parasol . This large canopy-like structure, 150 metres (492ft) long, 70 metres (229ft) wide and 26 metres (85ft) high, is part of a renovation programme for the once dilapidated Plaza de la Encarnación. The lower levels contain the Antiquarium (Archaeological museum; Tue–Sat 10am–8pm, Sun 10am–2pm), while elevators in the columns bring visitors to the rooftop for magnificent views. Seville's

The Torre del Oro, constructed in the 13th century

'other' futuristic building, the **Pabellón de la Navegación** (www.pabellondelanavegacion.es; Tue–Sat 10am–7.30pm, Sun 10am–3pm), resides on the Isla de la Cartuja. This architecturally impressive pavilion houses an ultra-modern navigation museum. Also worth a visit are the **Palacio de las Dueñas** (www.lasduenas.es), the favourite home of the late Duchess de Alba, and the **Hospital de los Venerables Sacerdotes**, which houses a fine collection of works by Velázquez and Murillo.

CARMONA

Carmona , 20km (12 miles) east of Sevilla on the road to Córdoba, sits like a beacon on top of the only hill on an otherwise unrelenting plain. That position has given it strategic importance during its 5,000-year history. It was the Roman era, though, that brought the area prosperity, and the **Museo y Necrópolis** (Tue–Sat 9am–6pm, Sun 9am–3pm; free) is the largest Roman necropolis outside of Rome.

The town declined after the Romans left, but the Moorish invasion of 713 brought renewed growth and prosperity. The Moors' reign ended in 1247 when King Fernando II reconquered Carmona. The town was divided among the victors, principally the orders of Santiago and Calatrava. The 14th and 15th centuries were troubled times as well. The discord was only brought to an end when, in 1630, Felipe IV agreed to grant Carmona the rights of township. The two gates that linked the old Roman road, the unusually shaped **Puerta de Sevilla** and **Puerta de Córdoba**, shouldn't be missed.

CÓRDOBA

These days, **Córdoba** ⑱, a minor provincial city sandwiched between Sevilla and Granada, is often passed over by visitors to Andalucía. But to do so is a considerable mistake. Besides being a very agreeable city, it has fabulous historic connections and an eclectic array of attractions to match. Córdoba was once the largest city in Roman Spain, the capital of the province of Batik and the birthplace of Seneca the Younger, philosopher and tragedian. Its golden era was between the mid-8th and very early 11th centuries, when it was the centre of the great medieval caliphate of Córdoba and one of the world's largest and most cultured cities.

Golden Age

In its golden age, Córdoba was home to half a million people – almost double today's population. It had the first university and street lighting in Europe, and a library containing more than 400,000 volumes.

The city is dominated by the greatest surviving monument from that period, the Great Mosque-Cathedral, known as **La Mezquita** Ⓐ (https://mezquita-catedralde

cordoba.es; Mon–Sat 10am–6pm, Sun 8.30–11.30am and 3–6pm, longer hours in summer), which has the distinction of being the oldest monument in day-to-day use in the Western world. Construction was begun in 786, but it was enlarged three times before attaining its present size in 987. It covers an area of 2 hectares (5 acres). Córdoba was reconquered in 1236 and two small Christian chapels were added in 1258 and

The magnificent pillared interior of La Mezquita

1260. In the early 16th century Carlos V decided to construct a cathedral in the centre of the mosque.

Several gateways provide access through the high wall surrounding La Mezquita, the most impressive being the monumental Mudéjar **Puerta del Perdón** (Gate of Forgiveness). Pass through it into the ceremonial forecourt of the **Patio de los Naranjos**, with its fountains and orange trees, to reach the entrance to the mosque. Inside, as your eyes adjust to the dim light, you will see mesmerising rows of columns extending into the shadows in every direction. Antique shafts of crystal-studded porphyry, onyx, marble and jasper – they seem to grow out of the paving stones like trees in an enchanted forest. The double arches overhead, striped in red and white, form a fanciful canopy of curving branches. At the far end, set in the southeast wall, is the splendid 10th-century **mihrab**, lined with marble and gold mosaics, and the **maksourah**, the enclosure where the caliph

The Alcázar de los Reyes Cristianos

attended to his prayers. In the central area of the mosque, restorers have exposed a section of the original carved and painted cedar-wood ceiling, which was covered over with vaulting in the 18th century.

The **Catedral**, found at the very centre of the forest of pillars, presents an over-powering contrast to its immediate surroundings. The understated simplicity of Islamic design – and lack of human images – is replaced with an ornate blaze of colour within which human images in either paint, stone, gilt or wood abound. Around the walls more Christian chapels line the perimeter of the mosque.

North of La Mezquita lies the labyrinth of narrow streets that makes up the **Barrio de la Judería** (Jewish Quarter). Some of the best restaurants and *tapas* bars in Córdoba are here. Sights to look for include the Callejón de las Flores (Alley of the Flowers), lined with houses built around flower-filled patios that are typical of Córdoba, and the 14th-century **Sinagoga** Ⓑ (Tue–Sun 9am–3.30pm; free for EU citizens) in Calle Judíos. It's a modest affair, just one small room, with a balcony for female worshippers. Córdoba's Jews helped the Moors to gain control of the city in 711 and they lived in peace under the caliphate.

The most illustrious resident of the neighbourhood was the 12th-century philosopher and theologian Moses Maimónides, and his statue stands a few steps from the synagogue in the square named in his honour, **Plaza de Maimónides**. Also here is the **Casa de las Bulas**, which contains El Zoco, a small craft market; and the renovated **Museo Taurino** (Bullfighting Museum;Tue–Fri 8.30am–8.45, Sat 8.30–4.30, Sun 8.30am–2.30pm; www.museotaurinodecordoba.es).

Northeast of La Mesquita on the Plaza Jerónimo Paéz, the splendid Renaissance Palacio Paéz houses the **Museo Arqueológico de Córdoba** **C** (Tue–Sat 9am–8pm, Sun 9am–3pm, mid-Jun–mid-Sept Tue–Sun 9am–3pm; free admission for EU citizens). Pride of place goes to objects from the palace of the Moorish city of Medina Azahara (see page 74), such as the bronze stag taken from a fountain presented by Byzantine emperor Constantine VII. The visit continues in the adjacent contemporary wing.

A Christian king, Alfonso XI, built Córdoba's **Alcázar de los Reyes Cristianos** **D** (Tue–Sat 8.30am–8.15pm, mid-Jun–mid-Sept until 3pm on weekdays, Sun 8.30am–2pm) overlooking the river southwest of the mosque. The ramparts offer a fine view over the old town and the river, the islets in midstream each occupied by a ruined Moorish mill and the ridges of the Sierra de Córdoba low on the northern horizon. The Catholic Monarchs received Columbus and planned the invasion of Granada while resident here.

Stroll east along the river, passing the **Puerta del Puente** **E** (Gate of the Bridge) and the Roman bridge itself, one of the most wonderful sights of Cordoba, especially at dusk when the lingering sun makes the stone glow golden red. Continue to the unusual **Plaza del Potro**, which gets its name (Square of the Colt) from the fountain in the centre. The square is home to two interesting museums: the **Museo de Bellas Artes** **F** (Fine Arts Museum; www.museosdeandalucia.es; Tue–Sat 9am–8pm, Sun 10am–3pm, mid-Jun–mid-Sept Tue–Sun 9am–3pm; free admission for EU citizens) and the **Julio Romero de Torres Museum** (www.

museojulioromero.cordoba.es; Tue–Fri 8.30am–8.45pm, Sat until 4.30pm, Sun until 2.30pm; mid-Jun–mid-Sept Tue–Sat 8.30am–2.30pm, Sun from 9.30am). The latter is devoted to a local artist who specialised in mildly erotic paintings of beautiful Córdoban women. Another cultural highlight is the **Centro de Creación Contemporánea de Andalucía, C3A** (www.c3a.es), a stunning building hosting artists workshops and exhibition spaces.

Eight kilometres (5 miles) west of Córdoba lie the ruins of the intriguing **Medina Azahara** (www.medinaazahara.org; Tue–Sat 9am–6.30pm, until 8.30pm Apr–mid-Jun, mid-Jun–mid-Sept until 3.30pm; Sun 9am–3.30pm all year; free admission for EU citizens). It was commissioned in 936 by Abd-ar-Rahman III in honour of his favourite concubine, Al Zahra (The Flower). Records indicate that building materials for the grand design were brought from Constantinople and various North African locations. Despite such auspicious beginnings, it had a short life; the palace was razed with the break-up of the caliphate of Córdoba in the early 11th century. For nearly 900 years, it was left in ruins and only in 1910 did excavation work begin. Today, reconstructions give some impression of the magnificence of this sumptuous complex of baths, schools, gardens and stately apartments, built on three terraces. A special tourist bus runs to the Medina (Tue–Sun 11am, also 10am Sat–Sun and 4.30pm Tue–Sat in summer) from Avenida Alcázar in Córdoba (book one day ahead at the tourist office).

ALCALÁ LA REAL

The road from Córdoba to Granada is, in many sections, rather dramatic, with mountainous scenery and olive groves (Jaén Province is the world's largest olive-growing area), dotted with little white-walled towns often crowned with castles. The last sizeable town before Granada, **Alcalá la Real** ⑲, was a Moorish fortified city from the early 8th century and remained a strategic

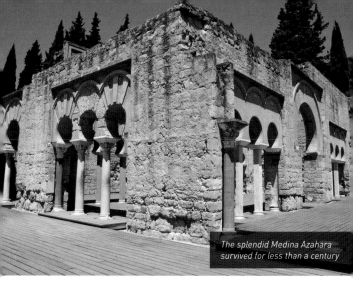

The splendid Medina Azahara survived for less than a century

bastion until the reconquest of Granada in 1492, after which further Christian monuments were added. The **Fortaleza de la Mota** (daily 10am–5.30pm, until 7.30pm Apr–mid-Oct), on the summit at 1,033 metres (3,389ft), is an amazing complex combining Moorish and Christian influences, and has fabulous views.

BAEZA AND ÚBEDA

Two handsome Renaissance towns stand on adjacent hills amid the olive groves northeast of the city of Jaén. **Baeza** is the smaller of the two and has a compact historic centre. Start your tour on foot outside the tourist information office in the Plaza del Pópulo, just off the main square. From here, go uphill towards the cathedral. The building opposite it is a former seminary decorated with elegant, calligraphic graffiti by its students. Heading back downhill you pass the Palacio de Jabalquinto, a magnificent palace with an exquisite Isabelline facade.

The mighty Alhambra towers over Granada

Úbeda ⑳ is an even more impressive repository of great architecture. Its finest buildings are by the architect Andrés de Vandelvira who worked for two wealthy noblemen employed by the king of Spain, Francisco de los Cobos and Juan Vázquez de Molina. The square in the centre of the old part of town is named after the latter of these, the Plaza de Vázquez de Molina. On it stands three remarkable buildings: the church of El Salvador, a mansion converted into a parador hotel and the Palacio de las Cadenas, now the town hall. Worth seeking out in the backstreets is the 14th-century Casa Mudéjar, housing Úbeda's archaeological museum.

GRANADA

The Nasrid dynasty rose to power in **Granada** ㉑ just as the fortunes of the Spanish Moors were beginning to wane. The first of the line, Mohammed ben Alhamar, established his capital here in 1232, after Fernando III had forced him from Jaén. Two years later, Moors fleeing from vanquished Sevilla swelled the population, which had already been augmented by refugees from Córdoba. Rather than grieve for the homes they had left behind, the industrious Moors set about making Granada the grandest city of Al-Andalus. Over the next century, the hilltop palace of the Alhambra took shape. Granada was the last of the great Moorish kingdoms of Andalucía to be reconquered, and King Boabdil's surrender to the Catholic Monarchs in January 1492 marked the end of the Muslim Empire in Spain.

The second most visited monument in Spain is the world-famous **Alhambra** and **Generalife Ⓐ** (www.alhambra-patronato.es; Apr–mid-Oct daily 8.30am–8pm, Tue–Sat also 10–11.30pm; mid-Oct–Mar daily 8.30am–6pm, Fri–Sat also 8–9.30pm). Entry is restricted to 6,300 people every day; advance purchase of tickets is highly recommended. This can be done online (https://tickets.alhambra-patronato.es) or by telephone on 858 953 616. Tickets can also be bought (if the daily quota allows it) from vending machines by the main ticket office. The Alhambra takes its name, which means 'the red one', from the red-brown bricks of its outer walls, which rise precipitously above the deep gorge of the Río Darro. Its strategically placed towers command superb views over the city below.

Within the walls of the Alhambra there are three main areas, which are best explored in the following order: the **Alcazaba**

Earthly paradise

In 1494, only two years after the Alhambra had been captured by Christian forces, the German historian, Hieronymus Münzer wrote: "There is nothing like it in Europe; it is so magnificent, so majestic, so exquisitely fashioned... that one cannot be sure one is not in Paradise."

(fortress), the **Palacio Nazaríes** and finally the **Generalife** (summer gardens). You need to allow at least three hours for a complete tour of the complex.

The Alcazaba is the oldest part of the Alhambra and only the impressive outer walls and towers survive. The main attraction is the view from the Torre de la Vela, north over the Albaicín and Sacromonte areas of the city and south to the high snow-capped peaks of the Sierra Nevada.

The highlight of the monument is the **Palacio Nazaríes**, the magnificent home of the rulers of the kingdom of Granada. It is actually a series of palaces, each with its own patios, fountains and other adornments. The intricacy, delicacy and sheer beauty of the design creates a visual impression beyond words.

The **Salón de Embajadores** (Hall of the Ambassadors), or royal audience chamber, is one of the most ornate rooms in the Alhambra. Skirted with geometric tiling, the walls and roof are overlaid with delicately shaped plaster stalactites, reaching 18 metres (60ft) to the carved and painted wooden ceiling. Verses from the Koran and the name of the 14th-century monarch Yusuf I are woven into the design. Through the tall, arched windows

◎ WASHINGTON IRVING

Irving was an American writer who is best known for *The Sketch Book*, a collection of stories that included such classics as *The Legend of Sleepy Hollow* and *Rip Van Winkle*. From 1826 until 1832, he was attached to the American legation in Spain, where he became fascinated by the legends of Moorish Andalucía. During his stay in Granada, he moved into the apartments of Carlos V while writing *Tales of the Alhambra*, a collection of stories about Granada's Moorish past.

are magnificent views of the Albaicín quarter and the River Darro. The hall exits into the delightful courtyard known as the **Patio de los Arrayanes** (Courtyard of the Myrtles), whose cooling pool is surrounded by myrtle bushes to increase the atmosphere of freshness; note also the arcade of graceful marble columns on the southern side. The **Sala de los Abencerrajes** recalls the aristocratic family of that

The beautifully landscaped Generalife

name, which was accused of disloyalty and collusion with the Christians by Boabdil. The king invited the Abencerrajes to a reception in this room and massacred all 36 of the unsuspecting family members. Also of particular interest are the **Patio de los Leones**, whose name derives from the splashing fountain in the centre upheld by 12 stone lions, the **Torre de las Damas** (Tower of the Ladies) and the old bath area.

The **Palacio Carlos V** is, as the name implies, relatively new and architecturally at odds with the more ornate older palaces, some of which were destroyed to make way for it. Commissioned by Carlos V in 1527, its square exterior belies a surprisingly elegant two-storey circular patio on the inside. Considered on its own merits, the building must be regarded as a fine example of Renaissance architecture.

Two museums are housed inside the palace. The first, the **Museo de la Alhambra** (Wed–Sat 8.30am–6/8pm, Sun and Tue until 2.30pm; free), displays such evocative artefacts as the throne of the Nasrids, a wooden armchair inlaid with silver and ivory, and the Alhambra Vase, which once graced the Hall of the Two Sisters. The second, the **Museo de Bellas Artes** (Fine Arts Museum; Tue–Sat 9am–6pm, until 8pm in summer, Sun 9am–3pm; free for EU citizens), contains works from the Renaissance to the 20th century.

The **Generalife** is found at the eastern end of the Alhambra fortifications on the neighbouring hillside. A modest summer palace, it is surrounded by beautiful terraced gardens where oleander and roses bloom luxuriantly and delicate fountains and cascades play among the neatly clipped myrtle hedges and avenues of cypresses.

Back down in the city, the most prominent monument is the exquisite **Capilla Real ⓑ** (Royal Chapel; www.capilla realgranada.com; Mon–Sat 10.15am–6.30pm, Sun from 11am; free on Sun with prior booking at www.arzo-bispadodegranada.com), a Renaissance chapel that serves as the mausoleum of the Catholic Monarchs. The effigies of Fernando and Isabel lie on the right-hand side of the chancel, with those of their daughter Juana La Loca and her husband Felipe El Hermoso on the slightly higher monument on the left.

Alley in the Albaicín

Their mortal remains have been interred in the crypt underneath since 1521, after being ceremonially transferred from the Alhambra. On exhibition in the **sacristy** are mementos of the Catholic Monarchs, including Fernando's sword and Isabel's sceptre and crown, a circle of gold embellished with acanthus scrolls.

Gypsy quarter

High up to the east of the Albaicín is the *Gitano* (Gypsy) area of Sacramonte, famous for its caves and *tablaos* (literally, stages), where Gypsies re-enact wedding ceremonies and put on flamenco shows. Tourists should be wary, especially at night, as this is not the safest part of town.

The adjacent **Catedral** **C** (http://catedraldegranada.com; Mon–Sat 10am–6.30pm, Sun and hols 3–6pm; free on Sun only with prior booking at www.archidiocesisgranada.es) next door is large and imposing. A few steps away is the **Alcaicería** area, the old silk bazaar of the Moors. These days, it's a colourful collection of narrow lanes with a concentration of outlets for handicrafts and souvenirs. Not far away is the **Corral del Carbón** **D** (House of Coal; daily 9am–7pm). Dating from the 12th century, it is the oldest Moorish monument in the city and is now a centre for typical Granadino arts and crafts.

The **Albaicín** **E**, the old Moorish district on the hill opposite the Alhambra, has a maze of narrow streets and staircases leading to ancient whitewashed houses and enclosed patios. Down by the Río Darro is the exquisite **Casa de Castril**, home of the Archaeological Museum (reopening in mid-2018; check www.museosdeandalucia.es), and the nearby 11th-century **El Bañuelo** (Moorish Baths). Further up the hill is the **Mirador San Nicolás**. From here, you get the best view of the Alhambra, with the majestic Sierra Nevada in the background – a scene replicated on countless postcards.

GUADIX

About 50km (32 miles) east of Granada on the road to Murcia is **Guadix** ㉒, a particularly unusual city in that many of its inhabitants are troglodytes. In the Barrio de las Cuevas are streets of houses with small front yards that are indistinguishable from ordinary homes. Look closely, though, and the white, circular chimneys emanating from the rocks give the game away. These are actually caves with a practical use: they're cool in summer and warm in winter. There is plenty more of interest here, including a Moorish castle dating from the 10th and 11th centuries and many important palaces, houses and churches.

LAS ALPUJARRAS

The **Parque Nacional de la Sierra Nevada** ㉓ has the distinction of having the highest peak on the Spanish mainland (Mulhacén is 3,482 metres/11,420ft high), as well as a wide diversity of flora made possible by the nearby Mediterranean Biosphere Reserve. It also has the highest road in Europe; along it is the Sierra Nevada ski resort, accessible all year round at some 2,500 metres (8,000ft), and Pico Veleta (Weathercock Peak) at 3,398 metres (11,148ft), which can only be reached in the summer.

Over the mountains from Granada, on the southern flanks of the range, is **Las Alpujarras**, a pretty area of steep hillsides and deep valleys dotted with towns and villages that retain more than a flavour of the traditional Moorish settlement. Their architecture of eccentrically shaped houses with flat gravel spread roofs sprouting eccentric chimneys takes you immediately back to a time when buildings were adapted to the contours not the other way round. Often houses cross over the streets and join each other, creating shady passageways and tunnels. The way of life here in the early 20th century was described by Gerald Brenan in his book, *South from Granada*. The Alpujarras were the backdrop for Chris Stewart's best-seller *Driving over Lemons*.

The main access to Las Alpujarras is from the Granada to Motril road, the same route along which the defeated Moors travelled on their way into exile. Even today, there is a pass 12km (8 miles) south of Granada that bears the sad name **El Suspiro del Moro** (The Sigh of the Moor). It is from here that distant Granada finally fades from view and it is said that the defeated King Boabdil sighed with regret as he looked back at the city. His mother apparently had little sympathy and is reported to have told him: "Don't cry like a woman for something you could not defend as a man."

Places to head for include **Trevélez**, the highest village in Spain, famous for its delicious *jamón serrano* (dried cured ham). **Lanjarón** is familiar throughout Spain as the name on the red, green and white label on bottles of water originating from the town's springs. Incidentally, that same water runs free from the *fuentes* (fountains) of many Alpujarras villages; some of the prettiest of them are **Pampaneira, Bubión** and **Capileira**.

Church belltower in the Alpujarras

Tarifa is world-renowned for its surf

WHAT TO DO

SPORTS

Many visitors to Andalucía stay in the Costa del Sol and plan for nothing more than lazing on the beach, perhaps saving their energy for the nightlife. However, sports facilities (see www.andalucia.org) are there in abundance for those who want to work off the effects of too much paella.

WATER SPORTS

The main resort beaches offer all kinds of sports equipment for hire, as well as beach umbrellas and loungers, and the larger beach restaurants have toilet facilities; some even have changing rooms.

Swimming. With more than 160km (100 miles) of beaches, the Costa del Sol offers plenty of spots for swimming. Most of the sandy strands lie to the west of Málaga, while shingle and rocks (with some sandy coves) predominate to the east. In the high season, the most popular beaches are mobbed. You stand the best chance of finding a patch of sand to yourself to the east of Nerja and west of Estepona.

Boating. There are numerous marinas along the coast between Málaga and Sotogrande, providing year-round moorings for yachts and motorboats. Some offer boats for day rentals and longer-term charters (with or without skipper and crew). Marbella has three such establishments and many of the beaches and larger beach hotels rent out sailing boats.

Waterskiing. The main resorts all have waterskiing schools, and most big hotels offer instruction. Prices are generally high, but they vary. Swimming and skiing areas often overlap.

Windsurfing. There's plenty of opportunity with boards, sails and professional instruction available in most of the resort areas. The season runs from March to November with the strongest winds in June and September.

Snorkelling and Scuba Diving. Snorkelling can be an engrossing activity, particularly off the rocky, indented stretch of coast beyond Nerja. If you dive or snorkel any distance from shore, you are legally required to tow a marker buoy. Diving centres operate in several resorts. For more information, contact the local tourist office (see page 130).

Angling. Fishing from the rocks and breakwaters is a popular pastime with local people and no permit is required. The deeper waters offshore teem with tunny (tuna), swordfish and shark. Deep-sea fishing boats can be hired at the marinas and

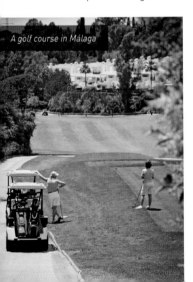

A golf course in Málaga

many resort hotels can make arrangements for fishing expeditions. A very popular inland fishing spot is the Pantanos del Chorro (*pantano* means reservoir) at the Chorro Dam north of Málaga. Freshwater anglers must have a permit – ask at the nearest tourist office for information on how to obtain one.

OTHER SPORTS

Golf. When it comes to variety, few resort areas in the world can compare with the Costa del Sol.

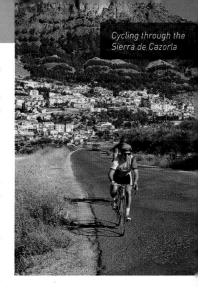
Cycling through the Sierra de Cazorla

There are over 90 golf courses and golf resorts in Andalucía (www.costagolfguide.com), around 60 of which are on the Costa del Sol. Most private and hotel clubs welcome non-residents or non-members, though some may charge visitors a higher fee. Clubs, caddies and carts are generally available for hire. The quality of the courses is excellent. Though a private club, Valderrama (www.valderrama.com), which has hosted the Ryder Cup, is open to the public between noon and 2pm (green fees are €350 on weekdays and €370 at weekends). For details of golf courses and fees, consult the website of the Spanish Golf Federation, www.golfspain.com.

Tennis. The climate of southern Spain is ideal for tennis and many hotels have their own courts for the use of guests. If yours doesn't, there is likely to be a municipal sports centre nearby with courts available for hire. The main resorts also have private tennis clubs where you can ask about temporary membership.

Cycling. Bikes can be hired at towns up and down the coast and inland (where mountain roads and trails are ideal for mountain-biking).

Hiking. There are a number of good hiking areas within easy reach of the coast, notably the Parque Nacional Montes

Siesta

The siesta is an afternoon nap taken to avoid the hottest part of the day. It means that many shops and businesses take a three-hour lunch break, closing from 1 or 2pm until 4 or 5pm, and then opening up again until 8pm. This age-old custom seems to be dying out in some parts of northern Spain, but it is still observed in the towns and villages of Andalucía.

de Málaga just north of Málaga and the impressive limestone formations of El Torcal de Antequera a little further inland (see page 55). For more good walks, try the area around Ronda, and the hills above the Refugio de Juanar near Marbella (see page 43). The E4 European Long Distance Path crosses Andalucía.

Horse Riding. Andalucía is famous for both horses and horsemanship. There are stables on the coast and near the inland cities, with mounts for hire; you can canter along the open beach or ride up into the hills.

Skiing. Skiing can be enjoyed between December and May at the Sierra Nevada Ski and Mountains Resort (http://sierra nevada.es) in the Sierra Nevada near Granada, 160km (100 miles) northeast of Málaga. Situated near the summit of Mt Veleta, it is Europe's southernmost ski resort.

SHOPPING

Most shops are open from 9.30 or 10am–1.30 or 2pm and from 5–8pm. The siesta (see box) is still religiously observed in southern Spain. But in summer, shops in the tourist resorts stay open throughout the day until 8.30pm or later. Department stores and supermarkets do not close for the siesta.

WHERE TO SHOP

The larger cities offer lower prices and a better selection of goods than resorts like Torremolinos or Fuengirola. The El Corte Inglés department store, with branches in Málaga, Sevilla and other places throughout Andalucía, is also well worth looking for.

For more sophisticated shopping, nothing can compare with Marbella or Puerto Banús, where dozens of attractive harbour-front boutiques offer a stunning selection of merchandise at equally stunning prices. You can make a considerable saving on luxury goods like jewellery, watches, perfumes and Havana cigars in duty-free Gibraltar, where there is no VAT (called IVA in Spain). Ceuta, the Spanish protectorate on the North African coast, has special tax status. Alcohol, for example, is vastly cheaper there than in mainland Spain.

MARKETS

Weekly open-air markets are held on Monday in Marbella, Tuesday in Nerja and Fuengirola, Wednesday in Estepona, Thursday in Torremolinos and San Pedro de Alcántara, and Friday in Benalmádena. Most cities have a *rastro* (flea market) on Sunday morning. The Mercado Victoria in Córdoba and the Mercado de Atarazanas in Málaga are both top gastro-nomic markets in Andalucía and well worth a visit.

Shopping for souvenirs in Albaicín district of Sevilla

Fans for sale

WHAT TO BUY

Ceramics. Everyday glazed terracotta pottery can be bought all along the coast. There is also a wide selection of tiles (*azulejos*), vases, bowls and jugs, with floral or geometric decorations in bright colours.

Foodstuffs. Take home a taste of Spain with some olives, olive oil, almonds, cheese or mouth-watering biscuits.

Jewellery. Silver rings, bracelets and necklaces in modern designs make good buys, as do the artificial Majorica pearls of Spain, fine filigree jewellery from Córdoba, and smooth, polished olive-wood beads.

Leather and Suede. Choose from a wide selection of handbags, belts, wallets, trousers, skirts, shoes and coats. Leather goods still compare favourably in price with Italian- and French-made articles, and the local factories turn out stylish, high-quality leather clothing. Córdoba is famous for its embossed leather. But beware: many of the leather goods you will see for sale have been imported from Morocco and are sold at inflated prices.

Souvenirs. Often delightfully tacky, from plastic castanets and flamenco dolls to imitation wineskins (*botas de vino*) and even bullfight posters printed with your own name.

Wine and Spirits. Sweet Málaga wine, sherry, brandy and Spanish wines provide some of the best bargains in Spain, and are generally cheaper when bought in a supermarket than at the airport.

ENTERTAINMENT

Tour operators offer any number of excursions with brochures and booking facilities available through your hotel or a local travel agent.

Bullfights. Andalucía is famed for its bullfighting traditions, and has two of the seven first-class *Plazas de Toros* (bullrings) in Spain (in Sevilla and Córdoba). The provincial capitals of Almería, Granada, Huelva, Jaén and Málaga, as well as Algeciras and El Puerto de Santa María have second-class rings. All others fall into the third class. The two main events are a *corrida de toros*, where fully qualified matadors fight fully grown *toros* (bulls), of at least four years old; and *novilladas*, where *novilleros* (novice matadors) fight *novillos* (adolescent bulls).

As a rule of thumb, the better events are held in the better plazas, particularly during the *ferias* (fairs) in the major cities. Equally true is the fact that most of the events held in the resort towns are mainly for the benefit of tourists and are of lesser quality – although they are not generally less expensive. Outside of the *ferias* – when they are held daily – only Sevilla has bullfights on a regular basis. In other places, with the exception of Easter Sunday and 15 August – important national holidays – they are held sporadically and advertised by way of the ubiquitous *carteles* (posters) stuck on every wall. The perceived cruelty of bullfights arouses very strong feelings among Americans and northern Europeans. They are, however, very much part of the southern Spanish culture. Visit www.andalucia.com.

Flamenco. All of the coastal resorts offer flamenco shows for tourists. They can be highly entertaining, but they are more in the spirit of show business than true flamenco. To experience flamenco at its most authentic, you will have to search out bars and small clubs in Málaga, Granada or Sevilla. Ask the local tourist office for advice on where to go (www.andalucia.org). For an authentic evening in Málaga try the Kelipé Centro D'Arte Flamenco (www.kelipe.net) performed in the 18th-century Palace Cropani.

Clubs and Bars. The Costa del Sol has one of the most thriving nightlife scenes in Spain (www.visitcostadelsol.com) and you will be spoilt for choice, from traditional bars to exclusive clubs. The area of La Nogalera in Torremolinos is a cosmopolitan, gay-friendly nightlife centre. Along with Benalmádena this is the hub of the 'open all hours' mentality and things don't really hot up until after midnight. There are hundreds of clubs in Fuengirola. On the other hand Málaga is a magnet for the chic and sophisticated night owl, with classy bars and pavement cafés, together with Marbella and glitzy, more opulent,

⊙ THE SOUND OF ANDALUCÍA

Flamenco is an ancient art form, combining elements of Visigothic, Moorish and Gypsy music. There are two distinct types; the *cante jondo* (deep song), an intense outpouring of emotion; and the animated *cante chico* (light song). There are also different varieties of flamenco dance, including the *tango*, *fandango*, *farruca* and *zambra*, performed to the staccato rhythms and counter-rhythms of the castanets, hand clapping (*palmadas*) and finger snapping (*pitos*), as well as furious heel-drumming (*zapateado*). There is no need to understand Spanish to enjoy the spectacle – you simply have to feel the music.

Puerto Banús. Puerto Deportivo in Estepona attracts a good mix of clientele to its lively bars.

Casinos. There are three gambling establishments that operate from 8pm to the early hours: Casino Torrequebrada (www.casinotorrequebrada.com) in Benalmádena-Costa, Casino Marbella (www.casinomarbella.com), under the Hotel Andalucía Plaza in Puerto Banús, and the much smaller

Flamenco in Córdoba

Casino Bahi de Cádiz (www.casinobahiadecadiz.es). Formal dress (jacket and tie for men) is required. Don't forget to bring your passport for identification.

Concerts. From May to October, Tívoli World (www.tivoli.es) brings the stars of rock and pop to Torremolinos for concerts in the open air. The season's programme may include performances of flamenco and *zarzuela* (Spanish light opera). In winter, the Málaga Philharmonic Orchestra performs in the Teatro Cervantes theatre (www.teatrocervantes.com). For classical music lovers, concerts at the Alhambra Palace in Granada are hard to beat (www.alhambra.info).

ACTIVITIES FOR CHILDREN

The Costa del Sol is an ideal place for families with kids – it is, after all, one long beach. Apart from paddling and sandcastles, older children can learn how to sail, waterski or windsurf. Alternatively, there are the **water parks** at Mijas and Torremolinos. Further diversions include the **aquarium** in Benalmádena (www.visitsealife.com), the Cueva (cave) de Nerja (www.cuevadenerja.es), **Mini-Hollywood** (www.oasysparquetematico.com) near Almería, Bioparc (see page 54) near Málaga and three Selwo parks (see page 36) (www.selwo.es). In the evening, **Tívoli World** (www.tivoli.es) near Benalmádena provides all the fun of the fair, with rides and a roller coaster, and there's a bar and flamenco show for adults. **Crocodile Park** (www.cocodrilospark.com), in Torremolinos, will intrigue most children, as will the horse show at **El Ranchito** (www.ranchito.com) in Benalmádena. Out in the country, get close up to wolves at Lobo Park (www.lobopark.com), an hour's drive from Málaga in the heart of Andalucía near Antequera. Other highlights to look for are the theme park on Cartuja Island in central Sevilla (www.islamagica.es), featuring pirates and knights, plus roller coasters and action rides, and the exceptional Parque de la Ciencias (www.parqueciencias.com) in Granada, where interactive displays and exhibitions bring science alive to all ages.

Children will enjoy a horse show

CALENDAR OF EVENTS

January: *Cabalgata de Reyes* (Three Kings' Parade), Málaga. On 5 January, the eve of Epiphany, floats, bands and traditionally costumed characters commemorate the visit of the Wise Men to the infant Christ.

March/April: *Semana Santa* (Holy Week), throughout the area. Sombre processions of hooded penitents and religious images every night during the week before Easter. Most impressive in Sevilla, Málaga and Granada.

April: *Feria de Abril* (April Fair, starts 10 days after Easter), Sevilla. Horses and riders, bullfights, flamenco, fireworks and street parties are part of Andalucía's most colourful festival.

April/May: *Feria del Caballo* (Horse Fair), Jerez de la Frontera. Spain's equestrian showcase, including racing, dressage and carriage competitions.

May: *Romería de San Isidro* (Pilgrimage of St Isidore), Estepona. Decorated carts and costumed riders parade. *Día de la Cruz*, Granada. Decorated crosses and folk dancing. *El Rocío* (Whitsun, May/June). Famous pilgrimage to a shrine on the edge of Doñana National Park.

June: *Corpus Cristi*, throughout the area. Bullfights and fireworks enliven this national holiday, a big event in Granada.

June/July: *Festival Internacional de Música y Danza* (www.granadafestival.org), Granada. Music and dance in the Alhambra and Generalife.

July: *Virgen del Carmen*, coastal towns. Processions of fishing boats pay tribute to the Virgin of Carmen, protector of fishermen. Festival Internacional de Música y Danza, Nerja. The town's famous cave provides the eerie venue for this subterranean celebration of music and dance.

August: *Feria de Málaga* (Málaga Fair; http://feria.malaga.eu), Málaga. A carnival, circus, bullfights and flamenco events enliven the first fortnight of the month.

September: *Feria de Ronda* (Ronda Fair), Ronda. The highlight of this fair is the *corrida goyesca*, a costumed bullfight. *Fiesta de la Vendímia* (Wine Harvest Festival), Jerez de la Frontera. A parade, bullfights, flamenco and equestrian events follow the blessing of the grape harvest.

December 28: *Fiesta de Verdiales*, Málaga. Groups from all over the province gather to celebrate this early style of folk song and dance.

EATING OUT

The big coastal resorts of the Costa del Sol are jam-packed with places to eat, ranging from hamburger stands to restaurants of almost any nationality you can think of. For those keen to sample the delights of the traditional Andalucían cuisine, there are also numerous fine Spanish restaurants throughout Andalucía, as well as on the coast. Go inland a bit and the prices drop considerably. Reservations are recommended for the more formal places. Lunch is generally served between 1.30–4pm and dinner between 9–11.30pm, although restaurants in the large resorts tend to serve meals all day.

WHERE TO EAT

One of Spain's most civilised institutions is the **tapas** bar, or *tasca*. Originally, the idea was that when you ordered a drink, generally beer or wine only, a small helping of a tasty morsel and a couple of pieces of bread were given free. The food was served on a small plate, traditionally used to cover the glass, and came to be called a *tapa*, which literally means lid. These days such authentic bars, with free morsels, are harder to find.

Cafeterías are middle-range establishments, common in the resorts, usually offering a selection of *platos combinados* (combination dishes), such as a

> ### Late eating
>
> First-time visitors to Spain are often surprised by the late eating hours: the Spanish rarely sit down to lunch (*almuerzo*), which is the main meal of the day for locals, before 2pm and dinner (*cena*) starts around 9.30 or 10pm. However, in the resort areas many restaurants stay open throughout the day.

Al fresco dining in Sevilla's characterful Barrio de Santa Cruz

pork chop and chips, or squid and salad, with bread and a drink included.

A **comedor**, literally 'dining room', is often a small area at the back of a bar where you can sit down and dig into a basic but satisfying meal. *Comedores* tend to cater to local workers: cheap and cheerful, they are usually open for lunch only.

Restaurantes are pretty much the same as anywhere else; they are usually open for lunch and dinner, and close during the afternoon and one day a week. They may offer a *menú del día* which will be much cheaper than ordering à la carte. A restaurant calling itself a *marisquería* specialises in shellfish and seafood, while an *asador* is the place for roast meats. A *venta* is a small, family-run restaurant serving down-to-earth country fare, and is well worth looking out for if you venture away from the coast. *Chiringuitos* are beachside restaurants that vary in size and quality.

WHAT TO EAT

Breakfast

Spaniards normally eat a light breakfast of cereal and toast or a *tostada con aceite* (toasted roll with olive oil) washed down with *café con leche* (milky coffee). Spanish espresso (*café solo*) is strong stuff, even with a touch of milk (*un cortado*). Resort hotels often offer a full buffet breakfast and, of course, a full English breakfast isn't hard to find.

Tapas and Snacks

Every good Spanish bar offers a selection of tapas. Among the dozens of items to choose from, you may find sweet red peppers in olive oil seasoned with garlic, Russian salad, slices

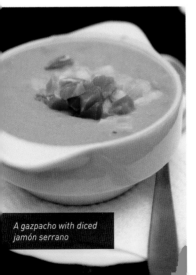

A gazpacho with diced jamón serrano

of sausage (both spicy *chorizo* and paprika-flavoured *salchichón*), *jamón serrano* (cured ham), marinated mussels, baby squid, clams or *tortilla de patatas* (Spanish omelette, with potato and onion filling, usually served cold in slices). For a larger portion of any given tapa, ask for a *ración*. If you feel that's too much for you, order a *media ración*. Late-night revellers often stop at a *kiosko* for a snack of *churros y chocolate* (doughnut-like fritters and

thick, sweet, drinking chocolate) on their way home.

Soups

Andalucía's most famous
speciality is the cold soup
known as *gazpacho*. There
are literally dozens of ways
to make it, but the version
you are likely to find in southern Spain is a chilled blend
of cucumber, tomato, and
crushed garlic, occasionally

Soup of the day

Be sure to try the mixed fish
or shellfish soups, *sopa de
pescado* and *sopa de mariscos*. Like its French coun-
terpart, the Mediterranean
bouillabaisse, sopa marinera
is based on the day's catch
and seasoned with tomato,
onion, garlic and a dash of
white wine or brandy.

accompanied by freshly diced green pepper, tomato, cucumber,
chopped hard-boiled egg and fried croutons on the side.

Originally from Málaga, *ajo blanco* (white garlic soup) is
a variation on the more common *gazpacho* theme. Ground
almonds and garlic form the base of this summer refresher,
served ice-cold with a garnish of almonds and grapes.

Vegetable Dishes

The Spanish usually eat vegetables as a first course, rather than
as an accompanying dish. Two good specialities of Andalucía
are: *alcachofas a la Montilla* – artichoke leaves cooked in a mixture of wine and beef broth, thickened with flour and seasoned
with mint, garlic and saffron; and *Judías verdes con salsa de
tomate* – green beans in tomato sauce laced with garlic.

Egg Dishes

Egg dishes make popular starters, and a whole Spanish omelette is a filling lunch on its own. *Tortillas* (omelettes) may
be filled with asparagus, tuna or mushrooms. *Huevos a la*

flamenca is a baked dish of eggs cooked on a base of tomato, garlic and herbs – usually accompanied by diced ham or spicy *chorizo* sausage, fresh peas and sweet red peppers.

Seafood

The seafood you are served in the waterfront restaurants was probably landed on the beach that very morning by the fishermen whose boats lie hauled up on the sand.

The traditional lunch on the coast is sardines skewered on a wooden spike and grilled over a charcoal fire on the beach. This simple but tasty dish is irresistible and extremely good value. Squid may be an interesting option, either cooked in its own ink (*calamares en su tinta*), a spicy dish, or simply dipped in batter and fried, and served with a twist of lemon. *Gambas* and *cigalas* are large juicy prawns – choose your own from the display and

⊘ PAELLA

Spain's most famous dish, which the Spaniards usually eat at lunchtime, deserves to be discussed separately. The main ingredient of paella is saffron-flavoured rice, cooked with olive oil, seafood and chicken. But every cook has his or her own variation on this colourful dish that originated in Valencia on Spain's eastern coast. The name paella derives from the flat, round metal pan in which it is cooked.

The secret of perfect paella is fresh ingredients; fresh seafood such as *langosta* (spiny lobster), *langostinos* (a kind of prawn), *cigalas* (giant prawns or sea crayfish), *gambas* (prawns), mussels, clams together with chicken or rabbit, peas, sweet peppers and artichoke hearts, all cooked together slowly as the rice absorbs the juices.

have them grilled while you select your wine.

Langosta (lobster) is excellent served hot with butter or cold with mayonnaise. *Boquerones* (fresh anchovies) and *chanquetes* (whitebait) are tossed in flour and deep-fried whole. *Boquerones* may also be prepared ceviche-style, marinated raw in oil and lemon with garlic and parsley. *Merluza*, or hake, may be served fried, boiled or mushroom-stuffed, per-

Traditional tapas bar in Sevilla

haps with tomatoes and potatoes. *Besugo* (sea bream) is a high-quality fish, which is brushed with olive oil and simply grilled.

Other common items on the menu may include *pez espada* (swordfish), *mero* (sea bass), *bonito* (tuna) and *rape* (monk-fish). If you have difficulty deciding what to try, you may want to plump for the *fritura malagueña*, a mixed fish fry that includes all of the above. Note that any of these delicacies are priced on the menu for a 100-gram (approximately 4-oz) portion, so what appears to be an inexpensive dish may prove very costly.

Chicken and Meat

Spanish chicken is delicious, whether fried, roasted or braised in white wine or sherry with almonds. The staple *arroz con pollo* (chicken with rice) is tasty. Many traditional meat dishes make use of offal such as tripe, brains and sweetbreads. *Riñones al Jerez*, kidneys sautéed with sherry, or *rabo de toro*, braised oxtail served in a rich tomato sauce with carrots and spices, are typical of the cuisine of Andalucía. *Ternera a la Sevillana*, veal in a sherry sauce with green olives, is a speciality of Sevilla. Rabbit (*conejo*) or hare (*liebre*) in white wine forms the basis of many a tasty casserole. Steak and various cuts of beef are also available. A local variation on this international standard is *bistec a la mantequilla de anchoas* (beefsteak with an anchovy butter sauce).

Cheese and Dessert

Spaniards eat cheese (*queso*) – notably the tangy *queso manchego* and the milder *queso de Burgos* – after the main course. You may also come across *queso de cabrales*, a combination cheese from the northwestern province of Asturias made from goat's, cow's and sheep's milk. After ageing, it becomes blue-veined and has a sharp taste similar to Roquefort. *Idiázabal* is a smoked and cured goat's cheese.

Fruits in season include *uvas* (grapes), *higos* (figs), *melón* (melon), *naranjas* (oranges), *melocotones* (peaches), *chirimoyas* (custard apples), *fresas* (strawberries) and *cerezas* (cherries). Besides ice cream, southern Spain offers pastries and cream desserts in abundance. One appealing preparation is *brazo de gitano* (gypsy's arm), a rolled sponge cake with rum-flavoured cream filling. The ubiquitous *flan*, or egg and caramel custard, appears on menus all over Spain. Eggs cooked with sugar make a thickened custard called *natilla*.

Wine and Spirits

The white wines of Rioja are very drinkable, but the Rioja reds are the glory of Spain; the aged Gran Reservas (at least five years old) are comparable to some of France's noblest red wines, though Riojas have a character all of their own.

Labels to look out for include Marqués de Riscal, Siglo, Cune, Berberana and Campo Viejo.

Navarra, north of the Ebro Valley, produces some interesting red wines (look for Campanas, Señorío de Sarría and Murchante). From La Mancha, between Madrid and Andalucía, come light, crisp Valdepeñas wines.

Reds and whites from Catalonia will also appear on wine lists. Labels to look for include Torres and René Barbier. Many restaurants have their own inexpensive table wine (*vino de la casa*) that can prove to be a less expensive, but still acceptable alternative. Catalonia also produces a sparkling wine, called *cava*. Some varieties may be rather sweet for northern palates but the Cordorniu or Freixenet *brut* (very dry) cava are both excellent.

Sangría, the iced combination of red wine and brandy with lemon, orange and apple slices, makes a great refresher, although its sweet and innocent taste can mask its strength.

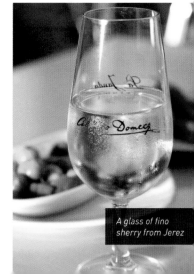

A glass of fino sherry from Jerez

An aristocrat among wines, *Jerez* (sherry) is produced from grapes grown in the chalky vineyards around Jerez de la Frontera. It is aged in casks by blending the young wine with a transfusion of mature sherry, a method known as *solera*.

Fino, the driest of sherries, is a light, golden aperitif that should be served chilled. A type of *fino* called *manzanilla* is slightly richer; Sanlúcar de Barrameda *manzanilla* is especially good. *Amontillado*, usually medium dry, is a deeper gold in colour, and is heavier than a true *fino*. *Amoroso* is medium sweet, with an amber colour, and *oloroso* is still more full-bodied. Cream sherries are not popular in Spain.

Andalucía produces several other semi-sweet to sweet wines, most notably the mahogany-coloured wine of Málaga, called *Málaga dulce* (rather like port). Sherry-type wines are also made in the Montilla-Moriles region near Córdoba.

Spanish brandy, or *coñac*, tends to be heavy, but it is usually drinkable and reasonably priced. The more expensive brands are much smoother.

Atmospheric bodega in Granada's Albaicín district

TO HELP YOU ORDER

Could we have a table? **¿nos puede dar una mesa?**
Do you have a set menu? **¿tiene un menú del día?**
I'd like a/an/some … **quisiera …**

beer **una cerveza**	milk **leche**
bread **pan**	mineral water **agua mineral**
coffee **un café**	napkin **una servilleta**
cutlery **los cubiertos**	potatoes **patatas**
dessert **un postre**	rice **arroz**
fish **pescado**	salad **una ensalada**
fruit **fruta**	sandwich **un bocadillo**
glass **un vaso**	sugar **azúcar**
ice cream **un helado**	tea **un té**
meat **carne**	(iced) water **agua (fresca)**
menu **la carta**	wine **vino**

… AND READ THE MENU

aceitunas olives	**judías** beans
almejas baby clams	**lenguado** sole
atún tuna	**mariscos** shellfish
bacalao cod	**mejillones** mussels
besugo sea bream	**ostras** oysters
bistec steak	**pastel** cake
calamares squid	**pimiento** sweet red pepper
callos tripe	**pollo** chicken
cangrejo crab	**pulpitos** baby octopus
cerdo pork	**salchichón** salami
champiñones mushrooms	**salmonete** red mullet
chuletas chops	**salsa** sauce
cordero lamb	**ternera** veal
gambas prawns	**tortilla** omelette
huevos eggs	**trucha** trout

PLACES TO EAT

We have used the following symbols to give an idea of the price for a three-course meal (without drinks), per person, including VAT:

€€€   over 40 euros
€€   25–40 euros
€   under 25 euros

BENALMÁDENA-PUEBLO

La Nina €€ *Plaza de España (corner of Calle Real), tel: 952 449 193,* www.aicorestaurants.com. In a lovely setting in the heart of the village, La Nina really delivers on flavour; the garam masala lamb is popular. Thu–Tue 10am–5pm.

CADÍZ

Balandro €€ *Alameda Apodaca 22, tel: 956 220 992;* www.restaurante balandro.com. A stylish restaurant and bar with a sea-inspired menu that highlights Cadíz Bay fried fish and tuna Asian-style. Meat, poultry and pasta feature, too. Daily L&D.

CARMONA

Gracia €€€ *Plaza de Lasso 1, tel: 954 191 000,* www.casadecarmona.com. The restaurant of the Casa de Carmona hotel (see page 135), set in the wonderfully renovated stables of this former Renaissance palace. The exquisite furniture, silverware and crystal complement the classically prepared international and Andalucían dishes. Daily L&D.

CÓRDOBA

Almudaina €€ *Plaza Campo Santo de los Mártires 1, tel: 957 474 342,* www.restaurantealmudaina.com. A restored 16th-century palace in the Jewish Quarter. Distinguished surroundings enhance the traditional Córdoban cuisine, prepared with fresh market produce. Mon–Sat L&D, Sun D

El Churrasco €€ *Romero 16, tel: 957 290 819*; http://elchurrasco.com. Seasonal cuisine and wines from their own Wine Museum, served in a 14th-century house in the Jewish Quarter. Daily L&D, closed August.

ESTEPONA

Robbies €€€ *Calle Jubrique 11, tel: 952 802 121.* Gathering fame since 1985, this slightly eccentric restaurant goes the extra mile. The host, Robbie, makes everyone feel special and the food never fails to impress. Tue–Sun D only.

FUENGIROLA

La Caracola €€ *Paseo Maritimo (Playa), tel: 952 584 687*; http://chiringuito lacaracola.com. This restaurant on the beach just south of the marina has a relaxed atmosphere and serves specialities such as seafood casserole, small fried fish and fish baked in salt. Daily L&D.

GRANADA

Chikito €€€ *Plaza del Campillo 9, tel: 958 223 364*; www.restaurantechikito. com. Typically Andalucían cuisine, a reasonably priced wine list and a city-centre location just south of the cathedral. Frequented by intellectuals and celebrities, whose photographs adorn the walls. Thu–Tue L&D.

El Mercader €€ *Calle Imprenta 2, tel: 633 790 440. One of* Granada's most popular restaurants, close to the Plaza Nueva in the heart of the town, it has a simple, quirky interior. Run by a husband and wife team, it offers exquisite traditional food and a great selection of wines. Wed D, Thu–Sun L &D.

La Yedra Real € *Paseo de la Sabika 15, tel: 958 229 145.* Located next to the Generalife gardens, this is a very pleasant modern restaurant with a nice terrace that offers typical Spanish dishes at very competitive prices. Tue–Sun 9.30am–5pm.

JEREZ DE LA FRONTERA

Tendido 6 €€ *Circo 12-14, tel: 956 344 835,* www.tendido6.com. Next to the Plaza de Toros, with bull-themed decor to match. Wide range of Andalucían cuisine and a mainly Spanish wine list. Mon–Sat L&D.

Venta Esteban €€ *Calle Ermita de Caulina 11-03, tel: 956 316 067;* www.restauranteventaesteban.es. Off the beaten track, this place offers a truly regional cuisine featuring local staples, such as sopa de mariscos and gazpacho andaluz, as well as delicious seafood and fish. Mon–Sat L&D.

MÁLAGA

Antigua Casa de Guardia € *Alameda Principal 18, tel: 952 214 680;* http://antiguacasadeguardia.com. Founded in 1840 and hardly changed since. Huge wooden barrels of local wines sit behind long wooden bars. Be sure to taste the small dishes of prawns, clams, mussels and other shellfish. Close to the Mercado Atarazanas. Cash only. Mon–Sat L&D, Sun L only.

El Chinitas €€ *Moreno Monroy 4-6, tel: 952 210 972.* Restaurant in the Old Town specialising in Andalucían and Málagueño dishes. Eat in or on the pedestrianised street in front. Daily L&D.

El Mesón de Cervantes €€ *Calle Alamos 11, tel: 952 216 274,* www.elmesondecervantes.com. Great tasting traditional and innovative tapas served in stylish surroundings by attentive staff. Wed–Mon D only.

Mesón Mariano €€–€€€ *Calle Granados 2, tel: 952 211 899,* www.restaurante-mesonmariano.es. Conveniently located in the heart of the old town, this quaint restaurant serves delicious regional dishes including chivo malagueño (Malagan kid), alcachofas (artichoke) and bacalao (cod). Daily L&D.

La Recova € *5 Pasaje de Nuestra Señora de Los Dolores de San Juan, tel: 952 216 794;* www.larecova.es. This tiny comedor cum artisan shop in the heart of the old town serves modestly priced, nonetheless excellent, breakfasts and lunches. Swift and friendly service. Expect queues, though. Mon–Fri 8.30am–4pm, Sat 8.30am–12.30pm.

MARBELLA

Chiringuito El Faro €€ *Playa del Faro, Paseo Marítimo, tel: 952 868 520;* http://restaurantefaro.com. A pleasant restaurant in the Pesquera chain. This one, on the beach, does great seafood and has a wonderful atmosphere. Daily L&D.

EL PUERTO DE SANTA MARÍA

El Faro del Puerto €€€ *Avda. de Fuenterrabía, Km0.5, tel: 956 870 952;* www.elfarodelpuerto.com. Surrounded by its own gardens, this restaurant is renowned for creative cuisine with traditional dishes, and an extensive wine list. Daily L&D, closed Sun D except Aug.

Romerijo €€€ *Plaza Herreria 1, tel: 956 541 254.* In a city famous for its seafood, this place, serving every variety of fish, is easily the most popular. Daily L&D.

SALOBREÑA

El Peñón €€–€€€ *Paseo Marítimo s/n, tel: 958 610 538;* www.restaurante elpenon.es. In a superb setting looking down over the sea, El Peñon specialises in seafood, especially from the barbeque. Steaks are popular, too. Daily L&D.

SAN FERNANDO

Ventorrillo el Chato €€€ *Carretera Cádiz–San Fernando, Km687, tel: 956 250 025,* www.ventorrilloelchato.com. On the isthmus connecting Cádiz to San Fernando, this is a historic restaurant with an attractive Andalucían-style dining room. It has Andalucían-style cuisine, too, with tasty desserts and fine wines. Mon–Sat L&D, Sun L (also D in August).

SEVILLA

La Albahaca €€€€ *Plaza Santa Cruz 12, tel: 954 220 714.* Housed in a typical Sevillana mansion near the Real Alcázar, La Albahaca offers three dining rooms and alfresco dining in summer. Basque-based menu with exquisite seasonal dishes. Mon–Sat L&D.

Casa Robles €€€ *Alvarez Quintero 58, tel: 954 213 150;* www.casarobles. es. This restaurant, in an 18th-century mansion close to the cathedral, is popular with locals and tourists alike. Traditional Andalucían stews and seafood dishes, as well as home-made desserts. Daily L&D.

Corral del Agua €€ *Agua 6, tel: 954 224 841;* http://corraldelagua.es. An attractive 17th-century house in the Barrio de Santa Cruz. Serves classic Andalucían cuisine. Seating available on a lovely patio around a fountain. Mon–Sat L&D.

Restaurante Oriza €€€ *San Fernando 41, tel: 954 227 254,* www.restaurante oriza.com. Located in a beautiful building opposite the Jardines del Alcázar, Egaña Oriza is renowned for dishes that combine Basque influences with Andalucían traditions. Spanish and international wine list. Mon–Sat L&D, closed August.

El Rinconcillo €€ *Gerona 40–42, tel: 954 223 183,* www.elrinconcillo.es. One of the oldest and most atmospheric tapas bars in the city, dating from the 17th century, close to the Metropol Parasol. A running account of your bill is chalked up on the wall. Daily L&D.

Río Grande €€ *Betis s/n, tel: 954 273 956,* www.riogrande-sevilla.com. This is a fine restaurant in its own right, and offers a tempting array of typically Spanish cuisine. But, located just across the San Telmo bridge, its huge picture windows also offer the finest views of the Torre de Oro and La Giralda in all Sevilla. Daily L&D.

TORREMOLINOS

Frutos €€€ *Avenida de la Riviera 80, tel: 952 381 450,* www.restaurante frutos.es. Reputed to be Torremolinos' best restaurant with an enclosed terrace and air-conditioning throughout. The cuisine is a meeting of Castilian grilled meats and Andaluz fish and seafood. Mon–Sat D, Sat–Sun L.

A-Z TRAVEL TIPS

A SUMMARY OF PRACTICAL INFORMATION

A

ACCOMMODATION (see also Budgeting for Your Trip)

If you are travelling independently, you will find a wide range of accommodation in Andalucía and the Costa del Sol. For more information check www.spain.info. By law, room rates must be posted in every hotel's reception area and rooms. Meals (including breakfast) are not usually included in this rate, and VAT (IVA in Spanish) will be added to your bill. The Costa del Sol remains popular in low season so booking well in advance all year is advisable. Longer stay visits can attract good discounts.

Establishments are graded by each of Spain's 17 autonomous governments according to the following system, with one of the following classifications plus a starred rating, depending on the amount, kind and quality of services offered:

Hotel (H): Rated between one and five stars. The most expensive option, topped only by Hotel 5-star Gran Lujo (GL), signifying top-of-the-range accommodation.

Hotel Residencia (HR): Same as a hotel, but without a restaurant.

Motel (M): Very similar to a hotel, but in reality these establishments are rare.

Hotel Apartamentos (HA): Apartments within hotels and rated the same as a hotel.

Residencia Apartamentos (RA): Residential apartments without a restaurant, rated the same as a hotel.

Hostal (HS): A more modest hotel, often family-owned and operated, and rated between one and three stars. Rates overlap with the lower range of hotels, eg, a three-star *hostal* usually costs about the same as a one- or two-star hotel.

Hostal Residencia (HSR): Similar to a *hostal*, but with no restaurant.

Pensión (P): A boarding house, rated between one and three stars, with only basic amenities.

Ciudad de Vacaciones (CV): A hotel complex with sports facilities.

Casa Rural: Country house offering bed-and-breakfast or self-catering accommodation.

Parador: A state-run hotel, often in a castle or other historic building. Advance booking is not essential but is highly recommended for the most popular *paradores*. For information and bookings in the UK, contact Keytel International, 156 Blackfriars Road, London SE1 8EN, tel: 0800 160 1013, www.keytel.co.uk. In Spain, contact the Paradores de Turismo, Calle José Abascal 2–4, 28003 Madrid, tel: 902 547 979, www. parador.es.

> I'd like a single/double room **Quisiera una habitación individual/doble**
> with bath/shower **con baño/ducha**
> What's the rate per night? **¿Cuál es el precio por noche?**

AIRPORTS (see also Getting There)

The Costa del Sol is served by Málaga's **Aeropuerto Internacional** (AGP) (tel: 902 404 704, www.aena.es), situated some 8km (5 miles) west of the centre of Málaga and 7km (4.34 miles) from Torremolinos. There is a bus service (A Express Aeropuerto; 7am–midnight) every 20–30 minutes to Málaga, Torremolinos and Benalmádena Costa (tel: 902 527 200, check www.emtmalaga.es for timetables), as well as a train service (tel: 902 320 320, www.renfe.es, follow the signs marked *ferrocarril*) to central Málaga (line C1) and the coastal resorts from Torremolinos to Fuengirola. Taxis can be found at the taxi rank outside the terminal. The journey from the airport to central Málaga or Torremolinos takes about 10 to 15 minutes, and about 20 minutes to Fuengirola.

Other airports with international flights serving the region are at Granada, Almería, Sevilla's San Pablo (for all Spanish airports tel: 902 404 704, www.aena.es/es/aeropuerto-sevilla/index.html), and Gibraltar (tel: 350 200 12345; www.gibraltarairport.gi).

B

BICYCLE AND MOPED HIRE

Bicycles can be hired in most resorts on a daily or weekly basis. Rates for mopeds are considerably higher. Insurance is obligatory and costs extra, and a deposit will also be required. A special motorbike permit is needed for machines over 50cc, and the wearing of crash helmets is compulsory.

> I'd like to hire a bicycle **Quisiera alquilar una bicicleta**
> What's the charge per day/week? **¿Cuánto cobran por día/ semana?**

BUDGETING FOR YOUR TRIP

Southern Spain is one of the cheapest holiday destinations in Europe. To enable you to estimate the cost of your holiday, here's a list of some average prices in euros. They can only be approximate, however, as prices vary greatly from place to place. Prices quoted may be subject to IVA, at variable rates.

Accommodation: Rates for a double room can range from as low as €40 at a *pensión* or *hostal* to as much as €1,000 at a top-of-the-range, luxury 5-star hotel. As a rule of thumb, a nice mid-range hotel will cost between €70 and €140. Some hotels may have three or four pricing seasons. For example, in Sevilla during the Easter Week celebrations and the subsequent *Feria de Abril*, rates can be double what you would normally be charged. Low-season rates can be considerably lower, as are rates for rooms booked well in advance online.

Car hire: Prices vary dramatically depending on whether you hire before your trip starts, whether you hire from a company in your own country or locally, how long you hire for, whether you want an automatic or manual transmission vehicle, and what insurance coverage you want – or are obliged – to purchase.

Entertainment: A cinema ticket costs around €6–9, a flamenco night-club (entry and first drink) starts at around €25, and a club from €10 to €15. Amusement parks cost around €20 to €26 per adult with discounts for children and for tickets bought online (up to 15 percent). A bullfight ticket ranges from €40 to €200.

Meals and drinks: In a bar, a Continental breakfast will cost around €5 per person. A three-course lunch or dinner (without drinks) will cost, per person; under €15 for the cheapest *menú del día* in a small bar or restaurant; €20–30 for a moderately priced restaurant; over €30 per person for a more expensive restaurant, while the best will charge €60 plus.

In a bar, a draught beer (*una caña*), or a small bottle will range from €2–2.50, a coffee around €1.50–3, spirits around €4, a soft drink from €1.50 and a glass of local wine about €2–5. Sitting at an outside table usually means you pay more for a drink than if you sit inside at the bar.

Shopping: Again, prices can vary substantially. By far the cheapest places are the large hypermarkets such as Alcampo o DANI where, for example, a can of San Miguel beer might cost around €0.40–€0.50. In a small corner shop or *supermercado* (supermarket) the same beer might cost about €1 and similar price differentials exist for most other goods.

Sightseeing: Tickets to the major sights, such as Sevilla's Real Alcáza and Córdoba's Mezquita cost around €10; and the Alhambra in Granada is €14. Admission prices for most museums, galleries, cathedrals, etc. are far more modest.

Sports: Per-day green fees for golf range from around €50 to as much as €200 at the top courses. Tennis court fees start at €10 per hour. Horse riding starts at about €20 per hour.

Taxis: Taxis are generally inexpensive, with a typical city-centre trip costing around €5. It's best to establish the rate for a long-distance journey before you depart. There are fixed rates, well displayed, for all destinations from Málaga's international airport (www.aena.es).

Train: The *cercanías* (local) line between Málaga and Fuengirola is a fast, clean and inexpensive way to travel along this part of the Costa del Sol. A return (round-trip) ticket costs €5.40, and a single ticket aboard the regional train from Málaga to Sevilla costs from about €15.

C

CAMPING

There are numerous official campsites along the Costa del Sol and throughout Andalucía. Facilities vary, but most have electricity and running water, and many have shops and children's playgrounds. Some even have launderettes and restaurants. Rates depend on the facilities available. For a complete list of campsites, consult the *Guía Camping*, (www.guiacampingfecc.com) available from the Spanish National Tourist Office and some local bookshops.

Camping outside of official sites is permitted, provided you obtain permission from the landowner. However, you are not allowed to pitch your tent on tourist beaches, in urban areas, or within 1km (0.6 miles) of an official site.

May we camp here? **¿Podemos acampar aquí?**

CAR HIRE (see also Driving)

Unless you plan to stay in one of the remote parts of the Costa del Sol, or are touring extensively, a car is superfluous to your requirements. In fact, if you are based at one of the popular resorts or major cities, having a car is more of a disadvantage than an advantage (it's hard to find places to park and there's always the possibility that your car will be broken into).

However, if you do decide to hire a car there are numerous international firms operating in the cities and resorts of the Costa del Sol, but it's wise to shop around as daily rates can vary enormously. Reserving your car before you leave home is usually cheaper. Sixt car rental (www.sixt.co.uk/spain) has outlets in Málaga airport, Málaga town, Marbella, Estepona, Sevilla, Jerez de la Frontera and La Línea, and offer very competitive prices.

Comprehensive insurance coverage should be considered a necessity, even if it doesn't come as part of the package. Theft from cars is all too common in this region, and extra coverage against the theft of the radio and other car parts and damage caused by thieves is very reasonable and seriously worth considering.

Normally, you must be over 21 to hire a car and you will need a valid driving licence that you have held for at least 12 months, your passport and a major credit card – cash deposits are high and are not always accepted. Visitors from countries other than the US, Canada and those in the EU may be expected to present an International Driver's Licence.

> I'd like to hire a car (tomorrow) **Quisiera alquilar un coche (para mañana)**
> for one day/a week **por un día/una semana**
> Please include full insurance coverage **Haga el favor de incluir el seguro a todo riesgo**

CLIMATE

Plenty of hot sunshine and cloudless skies are the rule on the Costa del Sol, and in most parts of Andalucía, too. But, there are seasonal variations worth noting when you choose your holiday. From June to September, very hot days with low humidity are followed by slightly cooler evenings; rain is a rarity. In April, May and October, daytime temperatures remain quite warm, but it can get cold at night. From November to March, sunshine can still be enjoyed, but may be interrupted by chill winds from the mountains and even rain – so be prepared.

Inland, the climate is different. The triangle between Sevilla, Córdoba and Granada is the hottest in Europe, with summertime temperatures often well over 40°C (104°F). As their name suggests, the Sierra Nevada Mountains near Granada see snow in the winter.

The average monthly temperatures for Málaga are:

		J	F	M	A	M	J	J	A	S	O	N	D
max	°C	16	17	19	21	23	27	29	29	28	23	19	17
min	°C	8	8	10	12	14	17	20	21	19	15	11	8
max	°F	60	62	66	70	73	80	83	83	79	73	66	62
min	°F	46	46	50	54	57	62	68	69	67	60	53	46
sea	°C	15	14	15	16	17	21	21	23	21	18	17	14
sea	°F	59	57	59	60	62	69	69	73	69	65	62	57

CLOTHING

From June to September the days are always hot and lightweight cotton clothes are the order of the day. During the rest of the year, a light jacket and a raincoat or umbrella will come in handy. Warmer attire will be needed in Granada and the Sierra Nevada during the winter. Respectable (i.e. modest) clothing should, of course, be worn when visiting churches, although women are no longer expected to cover their heads.

CRIME AND SAFETY

Spain's crime rate is similar to that of other Western European countries, so the usual precautions apply. All thefts must be reported to the police within 24 hours and you will need a copy of the police report in order to make a claim on your insurance.

It's a good idea to photocopy the relevant pages of your passport and airline ticket and keep them in a separate place from the originals. If

> I want to report a theft. **Quiero denunciar un robo.**
> My handbag/ticket/wallet/passport has been stolen **Me**
> **han robado el bolso/el billete/la cartera/el pasaporte.**
> Help! Thief! **¡Socorro! ¡Ladrón!**

your passport is stolen, your consulate should be informed (see Embassies and Consulates).

D

DISABLED TRAVELLERS

Throughout Spain there has been a concerted effort to improve disabled access to both buildings and public transport. The RENFE train service provides disabled facilities at its main-line stations and on its trains. Wheelchair accessibility is improving in Andalucía and all new public buildings are required to have proper access. Some older buildings and hotels may still be unable to offer complete access but many hotels have specially adapted rooms. Useful contacts include the Spanish Tourist Office in London (www.spain.info) and local tourist offices in the region.

DRIVING

Rules and regulations: Drive on the right, overtake on the left. Give way to traffic coming from the right. Speed limits are 50kph (30mph) in built-up areas, 90–100kph (55–60mph) on highways and 120kph (75mph) on motorways. A reflective yellow jacket for roadside emergencies must be carried in the passenger compartment of the vehicle. The use of seat belts (front and back seats) is obligatory. A red warning triangle must be carried. Motorcycle riders and their passengers must wear crash helmets. Spanish roads are patrolled by the motorcycle police of the *Guardia Civil*. They can impose on-the-spot fines for common

> Full tank, please, top grade. **Llénelo, por favor, con super.**
> Please check the oil/tyres/battery. **Por favor, controle el aceite/los neumáticos/la batería.**

offences including speeding, travelling too close to the car in front and driving with burned-out lights.

Road conditions: The old main road along the Costa del Sol, the N340, has been almost entirely superseded by a motorway, the A7, which runs from Algeciras almost to Almuñecar on the Costa Tropical and from Adra to Almería. The missing section in the middle was finally completed in 2015, joining the motorway from Granada to Motril. West of Málaga the coastal motorway can be very busy and there is a toll-paying alternative, the AP7. Other motorways link Málaga with Seville, Córdoba and Granada and Algeciras with Seville, Jerez de la Frontera and Cádiz.

Main ('N') roads in Andalucía are generally fast and good. In general, Andalucía is a mountainous region and there are long, winding stretches of road where it is essential to drive slowly. A few less frequented backroads are in bad state of repair. Signposting is of variable quality but the usual way to find your way around in Spain is to ask the locals.

Entering Gibraltar by car: If you arrive by car (Gibraltar is less than two hours' drive from Málaga), you have two choices, neither of which is ideal. It is easier and often much faster to leave your car in one of the car

> There's been an accident. **Ha habido un accidente.**
> My car has broken down. **Mi coche se ha estropeado**
> Where is the nearest garage? **¿Donde está el garage más cercano?**

parks in La Línea and cross the border on foot. Once you are in Gibraltar, a car is a hindrance in the town centre and only really useful if you want to take a tour of the Upper Rock. However, the downside of this strategy is the risk of having your car broken into in La Línea. If you want to take your vehicle with you, bear in mind that there may be long delays in either direction. Beyond the customs area, access to Gibraltar is across the middle of the airport runway (the road has to be closed when aircraft land and take off), then past the defensive walls to the town centre.

Fuel: Service stations are plentiful, but it's a good idea to keep an eye on the gauge in more remote areas, like the Alpujarras.

Parking (*aparcamiento*): Parking regulations are strictly enforced – offending vehicles will be towed away and a hefty fine charged for their return. A yellow-painted kerb means parking is prohibited at all times; blue means you must pay for a ticket at the meter to be displayed in your car.

If you need help: The Civil Guard is efficient with minor mechanical problems and go out of their way to help you if you have a breakdown. Spanish garages (*talleres*) are also efficient, but in tourist areas major repairs may take several days because of heavy workload. Spare parts are readily available for most major makes of cars.

Road signs: Most of the road signs used in Spain are international pictograms. But here are some written signs you will come across:

autopista (de peaje) (toll) motorway (expressway)
ceda el paso give way
circunvalación bypass/ring-road
curva peligrosa dangerous bend
despacio slow
desviación diversion
obras road works
peligro danger

prohibido aparcar no parking
salida de camiones truck exit
sin plomo unleaded petrol
Can I park here? **¿Se puede aparcar aquí?**

E

ELECTRICITY

220v/50Hz AC is now standard. An adapter for Continental-style two-pin sockets will be needed.

EMBASSIES AND CONSULATES

Australia: Level 24, Torre Espacio, Paseo de la Castellana 259D, 28046 Madrid, tel: 913 536 600; http://spain.embassy.gov.au/madr/aboutus.html.

Canada: Plata de la Malagueta, 2, 29017 Málaga, tel: 952 223 346; www.canadainternational.gc.ca/spain-espagne/offices-bureaux/consul_malaga.

New Zealand: Pinar 7, 3rd Floor, 28006 Madrid, tel: 915 230 226; www.mfat.govt.nz/en/countries-and-regions/europe/spain/new-zealand-embassy.

Republic of Ireland: Avenida de los Boliches 15, 29640 Fuengirola, tel: 952 475 108. Avenida de Jerez 21, Edificio Bayort, 41013 Sevilla, tel: 954 690 689; www.dfa.ie/irish-embassy/spain/about-us/the-embassy.

South Africa: Calle Claudio Coello 91, 6th Floor, 28006 Madrid, tel: 914 363 780; www.dirco.gov.za/madrid.

UK: Mauricio Moro Pareto, 2, Edificio Eurocom Bloque Sur, 29006 Málaga, tel: 952 352 300; www.gov.uk/world/organisations/british-consulate-malaga.

US: Avenida Juan Gómez 'Juanito', Edificio Lucía 1-c, 29640 Fuengirola, tel: 952 474 891; https://es.usembassy.gov/u-s-citizen-services/u-s-consular-offices/consular-agency-malaga..

EMERGENCIES

Unless you are fluent in Spanish, you should seek help through your hotel receptionist or the local tourist office. If you can speak Spanish, the following telephone numbers may be useful:

Ambulance/Police/SeaRescue
Spain 112/112/091/900202202
Gibraltar 112/112/199

G

GETTING THERE (see also Airports)

By Air. Spain's national carrier is Iberia (www.iberia.com), which has direct flights from London to the main Andalucían cities. British Airways (www.ba.com) has flights from London to Málaga, Granada and Gibraltar. The best fares, however, are always to be had by shopping around online between the many cut-price airlines, which now operate routes between various London and regional UK airports. These include easyJet (www.easyjet.com), Vueling (www.vueling.com) Jet2 (www.jet2.com) and Ryanair (www.ryanair.com). There are also many package holiday charter flights from Britain to Málaga, which roll transport and hotel accommodation into one price – if you buy at the last minute you may get a good deal.

By Road. From the UK, the main route from the French ferry ports runs south through western France to Bordeaux and into Spain at Irún, west of the Pyrenees. There are several possible routes to the south through central Spain, via Madrid and Sevilla or via Madrid and Granada.

Alternatively, take the route through central France to Perpignan and follow the A7 motorway south via Barcelona, Tarragona, Valencia and Alicante to Murcia. From Murcia continue to Puerto Lumbreras and take the A7/E15 to Almería and Málaga.

Your driving time (three steady days by either route) can be cut by using the long-distance car-ferry service from Plymouth to Santander or Portsmouth to Bilbao in northern Spain (see page 124). From Santander or Bilbao, follow the road to Burgos and proceed towards Madrid and the south.

By Rail. The best way to get to Spain by train from the UK is to take the high-speed Eurostar service (www.eurostar.com) from London St Pancras to Paris Gare du Nord. Cross the city to the Gare de Lyon to catch the double-decker TGV Duplex to Barcelona Sants. From Barcelona continue on the high-speed AVE train to Córdoba, Sevilla or Málaga.

International rail tickets can be booked through Rail Europe (www.raileurope.com)..

By Sea. From the UK, two companies offer car-ferry services to mainland Spain, with timetables varying by the season. Brittany Ferries (tel: 0330 159 7000, www.brittanyferries.com) has sailings between Plymouth and Santander (average crossing time 20 hours). They also have sailings from Portsmouth to Bilbao and Santander (average crossing time 24 hours). Motorists can then drive from Santander or Bilbao to Burgos and then continue south to Andalucía and the Costa del Sol.

GUIDES AND TOURS

English-speaking guides can be hired through local tourist offices (see page 130). Guided tours and excursions can be booked at most hotels or through any of the numerous travel agencies (*agencia de viaje*).

H

HEALTH AND MEDICAL CARE

Anything other than basic emergency treatment can be very expensive and you should not leave home without adequate insurance, preferably including coverage for an emergency flight home in the event of serious injury or illness.

Where's the nearest (all-night) chemist? **¿Dónde está la farmacia (de guardia) más cercana?**
I need a doctor/dentist **Necesito un médico/dentista**
I feel unwell **Me siento mal**
It hurts here **Me duele aquí**
I have a temperature **Tengo fiebre**
sunburn/sunstroke **quemadura del sol/una insolación**
an upset stomach **molestias de estómago**

EU citizens are entitled to free emergency hospital treatment. Britons need a European Health Insurance Card (EHIC, tel: 0191 218 1999, www.nhs.uk, or application form from the post office). You may have to pay all or part of the cost of treatment and medicines; keep receipts to claim a refund when you return home.

The main health hazard on the Costa del Sol is also its biggest attraction – the sun. Take the necessary precautions and avoid the midday sun. For minor ailments, visit the local first-aid post (*ambulatorio*). Away from your hotel, don't hesitate to ask the police or a tourist information office for help. At your hotel, ask the staff for assistance. *Farmacias* (chemists) are usually open during normal shopping hours. After hours, at least one *farmacia* in every town remains open all night. Called a *farmacia de guardia*, its location is posted in the window of all other *farmacias* and in the local newspapers.

L

LGBTQ TRAVELLERS

The gay and lesbian community in Spain has a high profile and the holiday resorts of the Costa del Sol are increasingly popular destinations. There are gay associations throughout the region, the largest and most well-known of which is Colega (www.colegaweb.org), with offices in Málaga, Granada, Córdoba and Sevilla. The district of La Nogalera in Torremolinos has become one of the most gay friendly nightlife areas on the Costa del Sol.

M

MEDIA (see also Websites)

Radio and television (*televisión*): There are several radio stations that broadcast in English on the FM band, such as Central FM (98.6 and 103.8; www.centralfm.com) and Talk Radio Europe (88.9 and 91.9; www.talkradioeurope.com). Radio broadcasts can also be picked up from Gibraltar. Network television programmes are all in Spanish, but the more expensive hotels and many British bars also have satellite TV with CNN, MTV, BBC, Sky TV etc.

Newspapers and magazines (*periódicos, revistas*): In the major tourist areas you can buy most European newspapers on the day of publication. The International Herald Tribune is also widely available as are all kinds of British and American magazines. The weekly Sur in English (www.surinenglish.com), available free, is aimed at residents on the Costa del Sol and carries local news and events. Other English language magazines and newspapers are published in different parts of the coast serving expatriate communities.

MONEY

Currency: The euro is the official currency used in Spain. Notes are denominated in 5, 10, 20, 50, 100 and 500 euros; coins in 1 and 2 euros and 1, 2, 5, 10, 20 and 50 cents.

Currency exchange: Outside of normal banking hours, many travel agencies and other businesses displaying a *cambio* sign will change foreign currency into euros. Larger hotels will also change guests' money. The exchange rate is slightly worse than at the bank. Take your passport when changing money, for identification purposes.

> I want to change some pounds/dollars **Quiero cambiar libras/dólares**
> Can I pay with this credit card? **¿Puedo pagar con esta tarjeta de crédito?**

ATMs: ATMs (*cajeros automáticos*) can be found almost everywhere, and from them you can draw funds in euros against your bank account with a credit or debit card.

Credit cards: All the internationally recognised cards are accepted by most hotels, restaurants and businesses in Spain.

VAT (IVA): Remember that IVA (*impuesto sobre el valor agregado*), the Spanish equivalent of value-added tax, will be added to your hotel and restaurant bills; it currently stands at 10 percent. A higher rate of 21 percent applies to goods and services, including car-hire charges, and a rate of 4 percent applies to certain basic necessities.

O

OPENING HOURS

Shops and offices and other businesses generally observe the afternoon siesta, opening 10am–2pm, and 5pm–8 or 9pm, but in tourist areas many places now stay open all day. Banks are generally open 8.30am–2pm, but will be closed on the numerous public holidays.

P

POLICE

There are three separate police forces in Spain. The *Policía Municipal*, who are attached to the local town hall and usually wear blue uniforms, are the ones to whom you should report theft and other crimes. The *Policía Nacional* is the national anti-crime unit wearing dark-blue uniforms; and the *Guardia Civil*, with green uniforms, is a national force with both military and civilian functions, whose most conspicuous role is as a highway patrol. Spanish police officers are generally courteous and helpful towards foreign visitors.

The emergency number is **112**.

POST OFFICES

Post offices (*correos*) handle mail and telegrams only; normally, you cannot make telephone calls from them. Routine postal business is generally transacted Mon–Fri 8.30am–8.30pm, and Sat 9.30am–2pm (main postal offices). Postage stamps (*sellos*) can also be bought at tobacconists (*estancos*), at hotel desks and at tourist shops selling postcards. Mail for destinations outside Spain should be posted in the yellow boxes marked *extranjero* (overseas); delivery is slow.

PUBLIC HOLIDAYS

Andalucía celebrates its regional holiday on 28 February, and banks, post offices, government offices and many other businesses are also closed on the following dates. Note that there are a number of local and regional holidays and saints' days too; check with the local tourist office.

1 January *Año Nuevo* New Year's Day
6 January *Epifanía* Epiphany
28 February Dia de Andalucía Andalucía Day
19 March *San José* St Joseph's Day
1 May *Día del Trabajo* Labour Day
25 July *Santiago Apóstol* St James's Day
15 August *Asunción* Assumption Day
12 October *Día de la Hispanidad* Columbus Day
1 November *Todos los Santos* All Saints' Day
6 December *Día de la Constitución* Constitution Day
8 December *Inmaculada Concepción* Immaculate Conception
25 December *Día de Navidad* Christmas Day

Moveable dates:
Jueves Santo Maundy Thursday; late March–mid-April
Viernes Santo Good Friday; late March–mid-April
Corpus Cristi mid-June

T

TELEPHONE

The country code for Spain is 34. To call the tourist helpline and emergency number dial 902 102 112.

In Málaga and other major towns and cities there are still a few phone booths for making local and international calls. Instructions in English and area codes for different countries are displayed in the booths. International calls are expensive, so be sure to have a plentiful supply of suitable euro coins. Some telephones accept credit cards, and many require a phone card (*tarjeta telefónica*), available from a tobacconist and some shops where you will see a sign outside. To call overseas, pick up the receiver, wait for the dial tone, then dial 00. Wait for a second tone, then dial the country code, area code (minus the initial zero) and number.

Remember, calling directly from your hotel room is almost always prohibitively expensive unless you are using a calling card. Very cheap telephone rates are available from Internet cafés and shops displaying a *Locutorio* sign.

Can you get me this number? **¿Puede comunicarme con este número?**

TIME ZONES

Spanish time coincides with most of Western Europe – Greenwich Mean Time plus one hour. In summer, another hour is added for daylight saving time.

| New York | London | **Spain** | Sydney | Auckland |
| 6am | 11am | **noon** | 8pm | 10pm |

TIPPING

Since a service charge is normally included in hotel and restaurant bills, tipping is not obligatory, but 10 percent can be added if service was exceptional. About 10 percent of the bill is usual for hairdressers and others offering personal services. In a bar it is customary to leave some small change to round up the bill. Tip porters 1–2 euros per bag, housekeeping in hotels €2–5 if you feel a good job has been done.

TOILETS

There are many expressions for toilets in Spanish: *aseos*, *servicios*, *baños*, *sanitarios*, WC and *retretes*; the first two are the most common. Just about every bar and restaurant has a toilet available for public use, but it is polite to buy a drink in the bar if you are going in there just to use the facilities. The usual signs are *Damas* for women and *Caballeros* for men, though you might also see *Señoras* and *Señores*.

TOURIST INFORMATION OFFICES

To assist you in planning your holiday, a great deal of information can be obtained from one of the international branches of the Spanish National Tourist Office (www.spain.info), as listed below.

Canada: 2 Bloor Street West, 34th Floor, Toronto, Ontario M4W 3E2, tel: 416-961-3131, e-mail: toronto@tourspain.es.

Republic of Ireland: 13–16 Dame Street, Dublin 02 HX67, tel: 353 0163 50 200.

UK: 64 North Row, London W1K 7DE, tel: 020 7317 2011, e-mail londres@tourspain.es.

US: 845 North Michigan Avenue, Suite 915-E, Chicago, Il 60611, tel: 312 642 1992, email: chicago@tourspain.es.

8383 Wilshire Boulevard, Suite 960, Beverly Hills, Los Angeles, CA 90211, tel: 323 658 7195, email: losangeles@tourspain.es.

60 East 42nd Street, Suite 5300, New York, NY 10165-0039; tel: 212 265 8822, email: nuevayork@tourspain.es

2655 Le Jeune Rd, Suite 605, Coral Gables, Miami, FL 33134, tel: 305 774 9643, e-mail: miami@tourspain.es.

For more detailed information about the Costa del Sol, contact the Costa del Sol Patronato de Turismo, Plaza de la Marina 4, 29015 Málaga, tel: 952 126 272, www.visitcostadelsol.com.

For information about Andalucía, contact Turismo Andaluz, Compañía 40, 29008 Malaga, tel: 951 299 300, www.andalucia.org.

For more detailed information about Gibraltar, contact the Gibraltar Tourist Board, Duke of Kent House, Cathedral Square, tel: (350) 2007 4950, www.visitgibraltar.gi.

For more information about individual cities and towns, visit the local tourist office (*oficina de turismo*). Offices are normally open 9am–7pm and all of them have somebody on staff who will be able to give advice in English. Major offices are located in the following cities: Granada, tel: 958 248 280; Sevilla, tel: 954 595 288; Málaga, tel: 951 926 020; Marbella, tel: 952 771 442/93.

TRANSPORT

By Bus (*autobús*): Buses are an excellent form of transport, not just along the Costa del Sol but throughout Andalucía. They reach many destinations that the train doesn't, and when they do serve the same places, they are often cheaper, faster and more frequent. Portillo Avanza (http://portillo.avanzabus.com) operates a service from Málaga that connects Torremolinos, Benalmádena-Costa, Fuengirola, Marbella, San Pedro Alcántara and Estepona. It also operates a service between Malaga and La Línea, a short walk from the border with Gibraltar. Alsina Graells Sur (www.alsa.es) operates daily services between Málaga and Sevilla, Granada, Córdoba and Almería.

> Where is the (nearest) bus stop? **¿Dónde está la parada de autobuses (más cercana)?**
> When's the next bus/ boat for...? **¿A qué hora sale el próximo autobús/barco para...?**
> I want a ticket to... **Quiero un billete para...**
> single (one-way) **ida**
> return (round-trip) **ida y vuelta**
> Will you tell me when to get off? **¿Podría indicarme cuándo tengo que bajar?**

By Ferry: Algeciras is a major port and Trasmediterránea (tel: 902 454 645, www.trasmediterranea.es) is the largest company operating from there. It has frequent sailings, on high-speed or regular ferries, to Ceuta, a Spanish enclave on the Moroccan coast, or Tangier, Morocco. It also operates a daily ferry on the much longer routes from Málaga (no service Friday) and Almería to Melilla, the other Spanish enclave on the Moroccan coast.

By Taxi: Taxis in the major cities have meters, but in villages along the rest of the coast they usually don't, so it's a good idea to check the fare before you get in. If you take a long trip, you will be charged a two-way fare whether you make the return journey or not. By law a taxi may carry only four people. A green light and/or a *libre* (free) sign indicate that a taxi is available. You can telephone for a cab as well. The numbers to call are as follows: in Benalmádena, tel: 952 441 545; in Estepona, tel: 952 802 900; in Fuengirola, tel: 952 471 000; in Málaga, tel: 952 333 333; in Marbella, tel: 952 823 535; in Torremolinos, tel: 952 380 600; and in Gibraltar, tel: 20070027.

By Train: A suburban (*cercanías*) rail service runs along the coast between central Málaga (Maria Zambrano station) and Fuengirola. It includes stops at the RENFE train station, the international airport in Málaga, Torremolinos and Benalmádena. Trains depart from Málaga every 20–30 minutes between 5.23am and 11.33pm. From Fuengirola, there is a half-hourly service between 6.10am and 11.50pm.

From the mainline (RENFE) station in Málaga there are services to Ronda, Córdoba, Granada and Sevilla, from where there are connections to other destinations in Andalucía. One of Europe's most scenic short rail journeys is the 80km (50-mile), single-track stretch between Algeciras and Ronda, which climbs steeply through the mountains. There are also long-distance (*largo recorrido*) trains via Córdoba to Madrid and Barcelona. Timetables and information are available from railway stations and tourist offices. RENFE has one information number, tel: 912 320 320, plus its website www.renfe.es.

Train Passes: For information on rail passes and tickets on Spanish trains, including the high-speed Euromed (Barcelona, Valencia, Alicante) or AVE (Madrid, Córdoba, Sevilla, Cádiz, Málaga) trains, American visitors should contact Rail Europe (tel: 800-622-8600, www.raileurope.com), *before* leaving for Europe; in the UK, contact Voyages-SNFC (tel: 08448 485 848, https://uk.voyages-sncf.com).

If you are resident in a qualifying European country you can get a single-country pass valid for three to eight days within a month. Prices are from £188. Alternatively you can buy a multi-country InterRail pass (www.interrail.eu) valid for 30 participating European countries including Spain. US visitors will need to apply for a Eurail pass, which gives unlimited first or second class travel for three to 10 days within a specified two month period. Adult prices vary from $240–607 depending on the class and the days.

V

VISAS AND ENTRY REQUIREMENTS

Most visitors, including citizens of EU countries, the US, Canada, Ireland, Australia and New Zealand, require only a valid passport – no visa, no health certificate – to enter Spain. Visitors from South Africa, however, must have a visa (obtained by contacting the Spanish embassy/ consulate before leaving).

WEBSITES

For general tourist information, look at:

www.spain.info Spanish National Tourist Office site

www.andalucia.org Andalucía site

www.visitcostadelsol.com Costa del Sol Tourist Office site

www.malagaturismo.com site for Málaga

www.marbellaexclusive.com site for Marbella

www.visitgibraltar.gi site for Gibraltar

www.granadatur.com site for Granada

www.turismodecordoba.org site for Córdoba

www.visitasevilla.es site for Sevilla

You could also try:

www.andalucia.com

www.malaga.eswww.legadoandalusi.es an organisation marking routes around Andalucía, in Spanish

The English-language publications *Sur in English* and *Costa del Sol News* have websites that have information about special events. Check out: www.surinenglish.com and costa-news.com.

YOUTH HOSTELS (see also Accommodation, Camping and Websites)

Red de Albergues Juveniles de Andalucía provides a complete listing of all youth hostels on the Costa del Sol and in Andalucía on their website www.inturjoven.com. Note that the Spanish word *hostal* does not mean youth hostel, but a basic hotel.

RECOMMENDED HOTELS

Our selection of hotels in Andalucía and the Costa del Sol are listed alphabetically by region or town – for each property we give a price category. As a basic guide we have used the symbols below to indicate prices per night for a double room with bath or shower, including service charge and taxes (but not breakfast), during the high season. All these hotels accept major credit cards unless stated otherwise. There are several categories of Spanish hotels; see page 112.

€€€€   over 200 euros
€€€   140–200 euros
€€   70–140 euros
€   below 70 euros

CADÍZ

Hotel Monte Puertatierra €€ *Avenida de Andalucía 34, tel: 956 272 111,* www.hotelesmonte.com. Beautifully designed modern hotel with a fine location, close to both the beach and old town. All expected amenities including on-site parking. 98 rooms.

CARMONA

Casa de Carmona €€€ *Plaza de Lasso 1, tel: 954 191 000,* www.casade carmona.com. A 16th-century Renaissance palace carefully and lovingly renovated into a beautiful and very hospitable luxury hotel, featuring a finely proportioned inner courtyard, airy breakfast terrace and the elegant Gracia Real restaurant. Every room is individually decorated and filled with handpicked antiques from Madrid, London and Paris. 33 rooms.

Cortijo El Triguero € *Carretera N-398 Carmona–El Viso del Alcor, Km18, tel: 917 251 037,* www.cortijoeltriguero.com. Found off the N398, just a short distance south from Carmona, this is a beautiful farmhouse surrounded by fields and a fighting-bull ranch. Expect traditional decor, a tranquil environment, good but unobtrusive service and a nice pool. 9 rooms.

CÓRDOBA

Hotel Casa de los Azulejos €€ *Fernando Colón 5, tel: 957 470 000,* www. casadelosazulejos.com. A 17th-century house, renovated in a Sevillana style, the Azulejos has a very interesting atmosphere. All rooms are set around a courtyard. Traditional decor, plus a bar, and a basement restaurant open Wednesday to Sunday with live music on Friday and Saturday. 8 rooms. Breakfast included.

Hotel Macía Alfaros €€ *Alfaros 18, tel: 957 491 920,* www.maciaalfaros. com. Just a short walk from the Mezquita, this is a dignified oasis of calm in the old quarter. Moorish in style, it has elegant rooms, a pool, restaurants and private parking. 144 rooms.

Hotel Palacio del Baílio €€€€ *Ramírez de las Casas Deza 10–12, tel: 957 498 993,* www.hospes.com. This palace, built over the ruins of a Roman house, was originally erected after the Reconquest in Córdoba. It also features stables, coach houses, lofts, granaries, Roman remains, valuable art and a grand garden, all of which have now been transformed into a beautiful hotel with modern facilities. 48 rooms, 5 suites.

ESTEPONA

Doña Matilde €€ *Revuelta 10, Cancelada, tel: 952 888 555,* www.hotel matilde.com. For something more traditional, try this good value family-friendly hotel situated at the foot of the mountains in the pretty village of Cancelada. Just 10km (6 miles) from Estepona, a few minutes' walk across the road to the nearest beach and 3 minutes' drive to El Coto de la Sirenca golf course. 19 rooms.

Grand Hotel Elba Estepona €€€€ Carretera Estepona, Km153, tel: *952 809 200,* www.hoteleselba.com. Located on the more recently developed western side of Estepona, but still close to the port, this stunningly designed hotel is a luxury destination with all the best in facilities and pampering. After relaxing in the superb spa or playing a round of golf, there are four excellent restaurants to choose from. 138 rooms and 64 suites.

Kempinski Hotel Bahía Estepona €€€€ *Carretera de Cádiz, Km159, tel: 952 809 500,* www.kempinski.com. The rooms in this recently renovated and architecturally interesting hotel all have sea views. There are also subtropical gardens, a 1km (0.6-mile) beach, numerous swimming pools, water sports, tennis courts, four restaurants and two bars.

FUENGIROLA

IPV Palace & Spa €€ *A7, Km207, tel: 917 763 373,* www.hotelipvpalace. com. Found just south of the castle, right on the beach, this is one of Fuengirola's best-located hotels. It also has a very pleasing atmosphere, a variety of pools and spa facilities. 285 rooms.

GIBRALTAR

Caleta Hotel €€€ *Sir Herbert Miles Rd, Catalan Bay,, tel: 350 200 76501,* www.caletahotel.com. The Caleta has the most dramatic location in Gibraltar, directly under the rock and overlooking the peaceful Catalan Bay on the least crowded side of the peninsula. Be sure to request one of the rooms with a delightful sea view. 160 rooms.

GRANADA

Al Andalus Apartments € *Calle Gracia 26, tel: 858 120 651,* www.al andalusapartments.com. This group, which also operates the Hammam Baños Arabes, offers apartments in the historic areas of Granada for 2–8 people. The prices are very competitive, but at certain very busy times there are minimum stays of 3–5 nights. 6 apartments.

Hotel Casa 1800 €€€ *Benalúa 11, tel: 958 210 700,* www.hotelcasa1800 granada.com. Located close to the Plaza Nueva, this is a beautiful 17th-century mansion complete with patios and galleries, and all the rooms are individually decorated. Parking is at the Plaza Puerta Real garage. 23 rooms and 2 suites.

Hotel Guadalupe €€ *Paseo de la Sabica S/N, tel: 958 225 730,* www.hotel guadalupe.es. Situated in the Alhambra complex very close to the palace, this comfortable hotel has a Granadino-style atmosphere. 58 rooms.

Hotel Palacio de los Navas €€€ *Navas 1, tel: 958 215 760,* www.hotel palaciodelosnavas.com. Dating from the 16th century, this building retains many original architectural features and is a charming hotel with a delightful mix of old and new located in the heart of Granada. 17 rooms, 2 suites.

Hotel Palacio de los Patos €€€€ *Solarillo de Gracia 1, tel: 958 535 790,* www.hospes.com. A large, classical, 19th-century palace right on busy shopping street in the heart of the city. The interior decor features a graceful and intriguing combination of the old and new. With its Los Patos Restaurant and Bodyna Spa, this is *the* luxury hotel in Granada. 32 rooms, 10 suites.

GUILLENA

Hotel Cortijo Torre de la Reina €€ *Paseo de la Alameda s/n, Torre de la Reine, tel: 955 780 136,* www.torredelareina.com. Located 12km (8 miles) from Sevilla, this attractive hotel is set within an ancient fortress and is surrounded by delightful large gardens. There is a good-sized swimming pool and activities such as golf and horse riding are available locally. 12 rooms.

JEREZ DE LA FRONTERA

Bellas Artes €€ *Plaza del Arroyo 45, tel: 956 348 430,* www.hotelbellas artes.net. A renovated mansion with individually styled rooms in the city centre near the cathedral and handily located for visiting other sights. There are lovely views from the terrace. 18 rooms (2 en suite).

Hotel Los Jándalos Jerez €€ *Nuño de Cañas 1, tel: 956 327 230,* www. jandalos.com. This stylish building, found between the Plaza de Toros and Avenida Alvaro Domecq, has uniquely decorated rooms, and a very colourful spa/hydrotherapy centre, which features a sauna, Turkish bath and hot tubs. 59 rooms including 2 suites and 17 duplexes.

Hotel Villa Jerez €€ *Avenida de la Cruz Roja 7, tel: 956 153 100*, www.
hace.es. Set in its own pleasant gardens, this charming hotel offers an
intriguing mix of traditional style and modern facilities. All of the rooms
look out over either the saltwater pool or the garden. 18 rooms.

LOJA

La Bobadilla €€€€ *Finca La Bobadilla, Apdo 144, tel: 958 321 861*, www.
barcelo.com. Set within its own large grounds, this complex, designed
to be a replica of an Arab village, is one of the most luxurious hotels
in Europe. Found between Sevilla, Granada, Málaga and Córdoba, the
huge rooms are stunning, and there is a gourmet restaurant, La Finca,
indoor and outdoor pools, the exclusive U-Spa with hydrotherapy pools
and treatments, and even a private chapel where you can get married.
26 rooms, 34 junior suites, 6 suites, 1 family suite, 2 presidential suites.

MÁLAGA

Casa al Sur € *Molinillo del Aceite 5, tel: 951 132 429*, www.casa-al-sur.
com. Cheap and cheerful, clean and bright hostel within easy walking
distance of all the main attractions, Shared or private rooms are offered,
plus roof deck, free Wi-Fi and complimentary tea and coffee. 8 rooms.

Hotel Don Curro €€ *Sancha de Lara 9, tel: 952 227 200*, www.hoteldon
curro.com. Well-established hotel on a quiet side street right in the centre of the city. The rooms have a pleasing mix of modern and traditional
decor and all modern facilities. Good value for money. 118 rooms.

Parador Málaga-Gibralfaro €€€ *Castillo de Gibralfaro S/N, tel: 952 221
902*, www.parador.es. A small *parador*-grade hotel beside the Moorish
castle on the hilltop above the city. The restaurant offers authentic Andalucían food, such as Malagan fish soup. Grand views over the city and
the bay. 38 rooms.

Room Mate Larios €€€ *Marques de Larios 2, tel: 952 222 200*, www.
room-matehotels.com. The Larios has an enviable position at the
heart of Málaga's principal pedestrian shopping street, adjacent to the

charming Plaza del Constitución. Unique in Málaga, the public areas and rooms have a delightful Art Deco design. Don't overlook the rooftop *terraza*, where you can enjoy the best views over the city. 41 rooms.

MARBELLA

Don Carlos Leisure Resort and Spa €€€€ *Avenida Zurita s/n, tel: 952 768 800, www.hoteldoncarlos.com.* Luxury hotel set in sub-tropical gardens on one of the best beaches on the coast, with views of Gibraltar and Africa; restaurants, bars, kids' club, spa, four swimming pools, tennis and 11 golf courses near to the hotel. 243 rooms.

Gran Meliá Don Pepe €€€€ *José Meliá s/n, tel: 952 770 300,* www.gran-melia-don-pepe.com. An imposing hotel just a five-minute walk from the city centre. Only tropical gardens and pools separate it from the beach. Every expected luxury can be found here, plus a health and beauty clinic, and several restaurants. 194 rooms and suites.

NH Alanda €€€ *Boulevar Principe Alfonso Von Hohenlohe S/N, tel: 952 899 600, http://alandahotelmarbella.com.* Located west of Marbella, close to the mosque, this hotel, surrounded by its own tropical gardens, has large and attractive rooms, some specially adapted for visitors with disabilities. It also offers a spa and wellness centre, and a poolside bar and restaurant. 196 rooms and 3 suites.

MIJAS

TRH Mijas €€ *Tamisa 2, tel: 952 485 800,* www.trhhoteles.com. In a superb location between the sea and the mountains, this hotel can be found in the pretty village of Mijas, 31km (19 miles) from Málaga. Surrounded by attractive gardens, the views are breathtaking. Facilities include outdoor pool, tennis court and sauna. 204 rooms.

EL PUERTO DE SANTA MARÍA

Hotel Monasterio San Miguel €€ *Virgen de los Milagros 27, tel: 956 540 440,* www.sanmiguelhotelmonasterio.com. An intriguing complex originally constructed in the 18th century as a Capuchin convent. The cells have been beautifully renovated. The Las Bovedas restaurant is located in the former monastery washroom. 175 rooms.

EL ROCÍO (COTO DOÑANA NATIONAL PARK)

Hotel Toruno €€ *Plaza Acebuchal 22, tel: 959 442 323,* www.toruno.es. Ideally situated in the historic town of El Rocío, this is a good place to stay when visiting the National Park. The hotel overlooks the lake where many species of birds can be identified including pink flamingos. The rooms are small but adequate and clean. You can eat at the restaurant Toruno just across the sandy street. 31 rooms.

RONDA

Hotel Polo € *Mariano Soubirón 8, tel: 952 872 447,* www.hotelpolo.net. A hotel located right in the city centre, and renovated in 2013 to combine a pleasing mix of the traditional and modern. The rooms are of a reasonable size and the staff helpful and friendly. This is one of the best value hotels in town. 36 rooms.

SEVILLA

Casa Romana €€ *Trajano 15, tel: 954 915 170,* www.hotelcasaromana. com. Close to the Sierpes pedestrian shopping street, this hotel has large, beautifully furnished rooms and public areas that include charming patios and the peaceful rooftop solarium. 26 rooms.

La Casa del Maestro €€€ *Niño Ricardo 5, tel: 954 500 007,* www.lacasa delmaestro.com. This beautiful mansion, close to the Casa de Pilatos, was once the home of the guitarist Manuel Serrapi Sánchez and the decor here reflects his interests. The rooftop patio offers spectacular views of the La Giralda. 11 rooms.

Las Casas del Rey Baeza €€€€ *Plaza Jesús de la Redención 2, tel: 954 561 496,* www.hospes.com. One of Sevilla's most prestigious hotels, with beautifully furnished rooms set around the courtyards. The Azahar

Restaurant reflects the flavours of Sevilla and Andalucía. Rooftop pool, Bodyna Spa and free use of bicycles. 41 rooms and 5 suites.

Hotel Husa Los Seises €€ *Segovias 6, tel: 954 229 495,* http://hotelhusa losseisesseville.spainhotels.it. A 16th-century palace blending historic surroundings with modern facilities to create an intriguing atmosphere. Central location in Barrio de Santa Cruz, tucked in behind the Cathedral. Rooftop pool overlooking the Giralda. 42 rooms.

Hotel Maestranza €€ *Gamazo 12, tel: 954 561 070,* www.hotel maestranza.es. The Maestranza is located just off the Plaza Nueva, between the Cathedral and the Plaza de Toros, in an impressive mansion typical of Sevilla. 18 rooms.

Petit Palace Marqués Santa Ana €€€ *Jimios 9–11, tel: 954 221 812,* https://en.petitpalacemarquessantaana.com. The Marqués Santa Ana includes all the high-tech features that are a speciality of this interesting hotel chain. Located close to the Cathedral. 6 high-tech rooms, 33 double rooms and 18 family rooms.

TARIFA

Casa Blanca €€ Nuestra *Señora de la Luz 2, tel: 956 681 515;* www.hotel casablanco.com. A delightful find in the centre of Tarifa, a hot destination for all kinds of surfing. Casa Blanco is a converted 19th-century townhouse with vaulted beamed ceilings and stone archways retained in rooms decorated with quirky modernity. A roof terrace and a café/ reading room complete the picture. 7 rooms.

TORREMOLINOS

Tropicana Hotel & Beach Club €€ *Tropico 6, tel: 952 386 600,* www.hotel mstropicana.com. Situated right on La Carihuela beach, the Tropicana has an interesting character and is set in its own small garden with a pool, beach club and the prestigious Mango Restaurant, which specialises in barbequed meat and fish. 84 rooms.

DICTIONARY

ENGLISH–SPANISH

adj adjective **adv** adverb **BE** British English **n** noun **prep** preposition **v** verb

A

abbey la abadía
accept v aceptar
access el acceso
accident el accidente
accommodation el alojamiento
account la cuenta
acupuncture la acupuntura
adapter el adaptador
address la dirección
admission la entrada
after después;
~**noon** la tarde;
~**shave** el bálsamo para después del afeitado
age la edad
agency la agencia
AIDS el sida
air el aire; ~ **conditioning** el aire acondicionado;
~ **pump** el aire; ~**line** la compañía aérea; ~**mail** el correo aéreo; ~**plane** el avión; ~**port** el aeropuerto
aisle el pasillo; ~ **seat** el asiento de pasillo
allergic alérgico; ~ **reaction** la reacción alérgica

allow v permitir
alone solo
alter v (clothing) hacer un arreglo
alternate route el otro camino
aluminum foil el papel de aluminio
amazing increíble
ambulance la ambulancia
American estadounidense
amusement park el parque de atracciones
anemic anémico
anesthesia la anestesia
animal el animal
ankle el tobillo
antibiotic el antibiótico
antiques store la tienda de -antigüedades
antiseptic cream la crema antiséptica
anything algo
apartment el apartamento
appendix (body part) el apéndice
appetizer el aperitivo
appointment la cita
arcade el salón de juegos recreativos

area code el prefijo
arm el brazo
aromatherapy la aromaterapia
around (the corner) doblando (la esquina)
arrivals (airport) las llegadas
arrive v llegar
artery la arteria
arthritis la artritis
arts las letras
Asian asiático
aspirin la aspirina
asthmatic asmático
ATM el cajero automático
attack el asalto
attend v asistir
attraction (place) el sitio de interés
attractive guapo
Australia Australia
Australian australiano
automatic automático; ~ **car** coche automático
available disponible

B

baby el bebé; ~ **bottle** el biberón; ~ **wipe** la toallita; ~**sitter** el/la canguro
back la espalda;

~**ache** el dolor de espalda; ~**pack** la mochila
bag la maleta
baggage el equipaje; ~ **claim** la recogida de equipajes; ~ **ticket** el talón de equipaje
bakery la panadería
ballet el ballet
bandage la tirita
bank el banco
bar el bar
barbecue la barbacoa
barber la peluquería de caballeros
baseball el béisbol
basket (grocery store) la cesta
basketball el baloncesto
bathroom el baño
battery (car) la batería
battery la pila
battleground el campo de batalla
be v ser, estar
beach la playa
beautiful precioso
bed la cama; ~ **and breakfast** la pensión
begin v empezar
before antes de

beginner principiante

behind detrás de

beige beis

belt el cinturón

berth la litera

best el/la mejor

better mejor

bicycle la bicicleta

big grande

bigger más grande

bike route el sendero para bicicletas

bikini el biquini; ~ **wax** la depilación de las ingles

bill v (charge) cobrar; ~ n (money) el billete; ~ n (of sale) el recibo

bird el pájaro

birthday el cumpleaños

black negro

bladder la vejiga

bland soso

blanket la manta

bleed v sangrar

blood la sangre; ~ **pressure** la tensión arterial

blouse la blusa

blue azul

board v embarcar

boarding pass la tarjeta de embarque

boat el barco

bone el hueso

book el libro; ~store la librería

boots las botas

boring aburrido

botanical garden el jardín botánico

bother v molestar

bottle la botella; ~ **opener** el abrebotellas

bowl el cuenco

box la caja

boxing match la pelea de boxeo

boy el niño; ~friend el novio

bra el sujetador

bracelet la pulsera

brakes (car) los frenos

break v romper

break-in (burglary) el allanamiento de morada

breakdown la avería

breakfast el desayuno

breast el seno; ~feed v dar el pecho

breathe v respirar

bridge el puente

briefs (clothing) los calzoncillos

bring v traer

British británico

broken roto

brooch el broche

broom la escoba

brother el hermano

brown marrón

bug el insecto

building el edificio

burn v (CD) grabar

bus el autobús; ~ **station** la estación de autobuses; ~ **stop** la parada de autobús; ~ **ticket** el billete de autobús; ~ **tour** el recorrido en autobús

business los negocios; ~ **card** la tarjeta de negocios; ~ **cent-**

er el centro de negocios; ~ **class** la clase preferente; ~ **hours** el horario de atención al público

butcher el carnicero

buttocks las nalgas

buy v comprar

bye adiós

C

cabaret el cabaré

cabin (house) la cabaña; ~ **(ship)** el camarote

cable car el teleférico

cafe la cafetería

call v llamar; ~ n la llamada

calories las calorías

camera la cámara; **digital** ~ la cámara digital; ~ **case** la funda para la cámara; ~ **store** la tienda de fotografía

camp v acampar; ~ **stove** el hornillo; ~site el cámping

can opener el abrelatas

Canada Canadá

Canadian canadiense

cancel v cancelar

candy el caramelo

canned goods las conservas

canyon el cañón

car el coche; ~ **hire [BE]** el alquiler de coches; ~ **park [BE]** el aparcamiento; ~ **rental** el alquiler de coches; ~ **seat** el

asiento de niño

carafe la garrafa

card la tarjeta; **ATM** ~ la tarjeta de cajero automático; **credit** ~ la tarjeta de crédito; **debit** ~ la tarjeta de débito; **phone** ~ la tarjeta telefónica

carry-on (piece of hand luggage) el equipaje de mano

cart (grocery store) el carrito; ~ **(luggage)** el carrito para el equipaje

carton el cartón; ~ **of cigarettes** el cartón de tabaco

case (amount) la caja

cash v cobrar; ~ n el efectivo; ~ **advance** sacar dinero de la tarjeta

cashier el cajero

casino el casino

castle el castillo

cathedral la catedral

cave la cueva

CD el CD

cell phone el teléfono móvil

Celsius el grado centígrado

centimeter el centímetro

certificate el certificado

chair la silla; ~ **lift** la telesilla

change v (buses) cambiar; ~ n (money) el cambio

charcoal el carbón

charge v (**credit card**) cobrar; ~ n (**cost**) el precio
cheap barato
cheaper más barato
check v (**on something**) revisar; ~ v (**luggage**) facturar; ~ n (**payment**) el cheque; **~-in** (**airport**) la facturación; **~-in** (**hotel**) el registro; **~ing account** la cuenta corriente; **~-out** (**hotel**) la salida
Cheers! ¡Salud!
chemical toilet el váter químico
chemist [BE] la farmacia
cheque [BE] el cheque
chest (**body part**) el pecho; **~ pain** el dolor de pecho
chewing gum el chicle
child el niño; **~ seat** la silla para niños
children's menu el menú para niños
children's portion la ración para niños
Chinese chino
chopsticks los palillos chinos
church la iglesia
cigar el puro
cigarette el cigarrillo
class la clase; **business ~** la clase preferente; **economy ~** la clase económica; **first ~** la primera clase

classical music la música clásica
clean v limpiar; ~ adj limpio; **~ing product** el producto de limpieza; **~ing supplies** los productos de limpieza
clear v (**on an ATM**) borrar
cliff el acantilado
cling film [BE] el film transparente
close v (**a shop**) cerrar
closed cerrado
clothing la ropa; **~ store** la tienda de ropa
club la discoteca
coat el abrigo
coffee shop la cafetería
coin la moneda
colander el escurridor
cold n (**sickness**) el catarro; **~** adj (**temperature**) frío
colleague el compañero de trabajo
cologne la colonia
color el color
comb el peine
come v venir
complaint la queja
computer el ordenador
concert el concierto; **~ hall** la sala de conciertos
condition (**medical**) el estado de salud
conditioner el suavizante
condom el preservativo

conference la conferencia
confirm v confirmar
congestion la congestión
connect v (**internet**) conectarse
connection (**internet**) la conexión; **~** (**flight**) la conexión de vuelo
constipated estreñido
consulate el consulado
consultant el consultor
contact v ponerse en contacto con
contact lens la lentilla de contacto; **~ solution** el líquido de lentillas de contacto
contagious contagioso
convention hall el salón de congresos
conveyor belt la cinta transportadora
cook v cocinar
cooking gas el gas butano
cool (**temperature**) frío
copper el cobre
corkscrew el sacacorchos
cost v costar
cot el catre
cotton el algodón
cough v toser; **~** n la tos
country code el código de país
cover charge la entrada
crash v (**car**) estrellarse

cream (**ointment**) la pomada
credit card la tarjeta de crédito
crew neck el cuello redondo
crib la cuna
crystal el cristal
cup la taza
currency la moneda; **~ exchange** el cambio de divisas; **~ exchange office** la casa de cambio
current account [BE] la cuenta corriente
customs las aduanas
cut v (**hair**) cortar; **~** n (**injury**) el corte
cute mono
cycling el ciclismo

D

damage v causar daño
damaged ha sufrido daños
dance v bailar; **~ club** la discoteca
dangerous peligroso
dark oscuro
date (**calendar**) la fecha
day el día
deaf sordo
debit card la tarjeta de débito
deck chair la tumbona
declare v declarar
decline v (**credit card**) rechazar
deeply hondo
degrees (**temperature**) los grados
delay v retrasarse

delete *v* **(computer)** borrar
delicatessen la charcutería
delicious delicioso
denim tela vaquero
dentist el dentista
denture la dentadura
deodorant el desodorante
department store los grandes almacenes
departures (airport) las salidas
deposit *v* depositar; ~ *n* **(bank)** el depósito bancario; ~ *v* **(reserve a room)** la fianza
desert el desierto
dessert el postre
detergent el detergente
develop *v* **(film)** revelar
diabetic diabético
dial *v* marcar
diamond el diamante
diaper el pañal
diarrhea la diarrea
diesel el diesel
difficult difícil
digital digital; ~ **camera** la cámara digital; ~ **photos** las fotos digitales; ~ **prints** las fotos digitales
dining room el comedor
dinner la cena
direction la dirección
dirty sucio
disabled discapacitado; ~ **accessible**

[BE] el acceso para discapacitados
discharge (bodily fluid) la secreción
disconnect (computer) desconectar
discount el descuento
dish (kitchen) el plato; ~**washer** el lavavajillas; ~**washing liquid** el líquido lavavajillas
display *v* mostrar; ~ **case** la vitrina
disposable desechable; ~ **razor** la cuchilla desechable
dive *v* bucear
diving equipment el equipo de buceo
divorce *v* divorciar
dizzy mareado
doctor el médico
doll la muñeca
dollar (U.S.) el dólar
domestic nacional; ~ **flight** el vuelo nacional
door la puerta
dormitory el dormitorio
double bed la cama de matrimonio
downtown el centro
dozen la docena
drag lift el telesquí
dress (piece of clothing) el vestido; ~ **code** las normas de vestuario
drink *v* beber; ~ *n* la bebida; ~ **menu** la carta de bebidas;

~**ing water** el agua potable
drive *v* conducir
driver's license number el número de permiso de conducir
drop (medicine) la gota
drowsiness la somnolencia
dry cleaner la tintorería
dubbed doblada
during durante
duty (tax) el impuesto; ~**-free** libre de impuestos
DVD el DVD

E

ear la oreja; ~**ache** el dolor de oído
earlier más temprano
early temprano
earrings los pendientes
east el este
easy fácil
eat *v* comer
economy class la clase económica
elbow el codo
electric outlet el enchufe eléctrico
elevator el ascensor
e-mail *v* enviar un correo electrónico; ~ *n* el correo electrónico; ~ **address** la dirección de correo electrónico
emergency la emergencia; ~ **exit** la salida de urgencia

empty *v* vaciar
enamel (jewelry) el esmalte
end *v* terminar
English el inglés
engrave *v* grabar
enjoy *v* disfrutar
enter *v* entrar
entertainment el entretenimiento
entrance la entrada
envelope el sobre
equipment el equipo
escalators las escaleras mecánicas
e-ticket el billete electrónico
EU resident el/la residente de la UE
euro el euro
evening la noche
excess el exceso
exchange *v* **(money)** cambiar; ~ *v* **(goods)** devolver; ~ *n* **(place)** la casa de cambio; ~ **rate** el tipo de cambio
excursion la excursión
excuse *v* **(to get past)** pedir perdón; ~ *v* **(to get attention)** disculparse
exhausted agotado
exit *v* salir; ~ *n* la salida
expensive caro
expert (skill level) experto
exposure (film) la foto
express rápido; ~ **bus** el autobús rápido; ~ **train** el tren rápido

extension (phone) la extensión
extra adicional; **~ large** equis ele (XL)
extract v (tooth) extraer
eye el ojo
eyebrow wax la depilación de cejas

F

face la cara
facial la limpieza de cutis
family la familia
fan (appliance) el ventilador; **~ (souvenir)** el abanico
far lejos; **~-sighted** hipermétrope
farm la granja
fast rápido; **~ food** la comida rápida
faster más rápido
fat free sin grasa
father el padre
fax v enviar un fax; **~** n el fax; **~ number** el número de fax
fee la tasa
feed v alimentar
ferry el ferry
fever la fiebre
field (sports) el campo
fill v llenar; **~ out** v (form) rellenar
filling (tooth) el empaste
film (camera) el carrete
fine (fee for breaking law) la multa

finger el dedo; **~nail** la uña del dedo
fire fuego; **~ department** los bomberos; **~ door** la puerta de incendios
first primero; **~ class** la primera clase
fit (clothing) quedar bien
fitting room el probador
fix v (repair) reparar
flashlight la linterna
flight el vuelo
floor el suelo
flower la flor
folk music la música folk
food la comida
foot el pie
football [BE] el fútbol
for para/por
forecast el pronóstico
forest el bosque
fork el tenedor
form el formulario
formula (baby) la fórmula infantil
fort el fuerte
fountain la fuente
free gratuito
freezer el congelador
fresh fresco
friend el amigo
frying pan la sartén
full completo; **~-service** el servicio completo; **~-time** a tiempo completo

G

game el partido
garage (parking) el garaje; **~ (repair)** el taller
garbage bag la bolsa de basura
gas la gasolina; **~ station** la gasolinera
gate (airport) la puerta
gay gay; **~ bar** el bar gay; **~ club** la discoteca gay
gel (hair) la gomina
get to v ir a
get off v (a train/bus/ subway) bajarse
gift el regalo; **~ shop** la tienda de regalos
girl la niña; **~friend** la novia
give v dar
glass (drinking) el vaso; **~ (material)** el vidrio
glasses las gafas
go v (somewhere) ir a
gold el oro
golf golf; **~ course** el campo de golf; **~ tournament** el torneo de golf
good n el producto; **~** adj bueno; **~ afternoon** buenas tardes; **~ evening** buenas noches; **~ morning** buenos días; **~bye** adiós
gram el gramo
grandchild el nieto

grandparent el abuelo
gray gris
green verde
grocery store el supermercado
ground la tierra; **~ floor** la planta baja; **~cloth** la tela impermeable
group el grupo
guide el guía; **~ book** la guía; **~ dog** el perro guía
gym el gimnasio
gynecologist el ginecólogo

H

hair el pelo; **~ dryer** el secador de pelo; **~ salon** la peluquería; **~brush** el cepillo de pelo; **~cut** el corte de pelo; **~spray** la laca; **~style** el peinado; **~stylist** el estilista
half medio; **~ hour** la media hora; **~-kilo** el medio kilo
hammer el martillo
hand la mano; **~ luggage** el equipaje de mano; **~bag [BE]** el bolso
handicapped discapacitado; **~-accessible** el acceso para discapacitados
hangover la resaca
happy feliz
hat el sombrero
have v tener

head (body part) la cabeza; **~ache** el dolor de cabeza; **~phones** los cascos
health la salud; **~ food store** la tienda de alimentos naturales
heart el corazón; **~ condition** padecer del corazón
heat v calentar; **~** n el calor
heater [heating BE] la calefacción
hello hola
helmet el casco
help v ayudar; **~** n la ayuda
here aquí
hi hola
high alto; **~chair** la trona; **~way** la autopista
hiking boots las botas de montaña
hill la colina
hire v [BE] alquilar; **~ car [BE]** el coche de alquiler
hitchhike v hacer autostop
hockey el hockey
holiday [BE] las vacaciones
horse track el hipódromo
hospital el hospital
hostel el albergue
hot (temperature) caliente; **~ (spicy)** picante; **~ spring** el agua termale; **~ water** el

agua caliente
hotel el hotel
hour la hora
house la casa; **~hold goods** los artículos para el hogar; **~keeping services** el servicio de limpieza de habitaciones
how (question) cómo; **~ much (question)** cuánto cuesta
hug v abrazar
hungry hambriento
hurt (have pain) tener dolor
husband el marido

I

ibuprofen el ibuprofeno
ice el hielo; **~ hockey** el hockey sobre hielo
icy adj helado
identification el documento de identidad
ill v (to feel) encontrarse mal
in dentro
include v incluir
indoor pool la piscina cubierta
inexpensive barato
infected infectado
information (phone) el número de teléfono de información; **~ desk** el mostrador de información
insect el insecto; **~ bite** la picadura de

insecto; **~ repellent** el repelente de insectos
insert v introducir
insomnia el insomnio
instant message el mensaje instantáneo
insulin la insulina
insurance el seguro; **~ card** la tarjeta de seguro; **~ company** la compañía de seguros
interesting interesante
intermediate el nivel intermedio
international (airport area) internacional; **~ flight** el vuelo internacional; **~ student card** la tarjeta internacional de estudiante
internet la internet; **~ cafe** el cibercafé; **~ service** el servicio de internet; **wireless** el acceso inalámbrico
interpreter el/la intérprete
intersection el cruce
intestine el intestino
introduce v presentar
invoice [BE] la factura
Ireland Irlanda
Irish irlandés
iron v planchar; **~** n (clothes) la plancha
Italian italiano

J

jacket la chaqueta
jar el bote

jaw la mandíbula
jazz el jazz; **~ club** el club de jazz
jeans los vaqueros
jet ski la moto acuática
jeweler la joyería
jewelry las joyas
join v acompañar a
joint (body part) la articulación

K

key la llave; **~ card** la llave electrónica; **~ ring** el llavero
kiddie pool la piscina infantil
kidney (body part) el riñón
kilo el kilo; **~gram** el kilogramo; **~meter** el kilómetro
kiss v besar
kitchen la cocina; **~ foil [BE]** el papel de aluminio
knee la rodilla
knife el cuchillo

L

lace el encaje
lactose intolerant alérgico a la lactosa
lake el lago
large grande; **~er** más grande
last último
late (time) tarde; **~er** más tarde
launderette [BE] la lavandería
laundromat la lavandería

laundry la colada; **~ facility** la lavandería; **~ service** el servicio de lavandería

lawyer el abogado

leather el cuero

to leave v salir

left (direction) la izquierda

leg la pierna

lens la lente

less menos

lesson la lección

letter la carta

library la biblioteca

life la vida; **~ jacket** el chaleco salvavidas; **~guard** el socorrista

lift n [BE] el ascensor; **~** v **(to give a ride)** llevar en coche; **~ pass** el pase de acceso a los remontes

light n **(overhead)** la luz; **~** v **(cigarette)** dar fuego; **~bulb** la bombilla

lighter el mechero

like v gustar; **I like** me gusta

line (train) la línea

linen el lino

lip el labio

liquor store la tienda de bebidas alcohólicas

liter el litro

little pequeño

live v vivir

liver (body part) el hígado

loafers los mocasines

local de la zona

lock v cerrar; **~** n el cerrojo

locker la taquilla

log on v **(computer)** iniciar sesión

log off v **(computer)** cerrar sesión

long largo; **~ sleeves** las mangas largas; **~-sighted** [BE] hipermétrope

look v mirar

lose v **(something)** perder

lost perdido; **~ and found** la oficina de objetos perdidos

lotion la crema hidratante

louder más alto

love v querer; **~** n el amor

low bajo; **~er** más bajo

luggage el equipaje; **~ cart** el carrito de equipaje; **~ locker** la consigna automática; **~ ticket** el talón de equipaje; **hand ~** [BE] el equipaje de mano

lunch la comida

lung el pulmón

M

magazine la revista

magnificent magnífico

mail v enviar por correo; **~** n el correo; **~box** el buzón de correo

main principal; **~**

attractions los principales sitios de interés; **~ course** el plato principal

make up a prescription v [BE] despachar medicamentos

mall el centro comercial

man el hombre

manager el gerente

manicure la manicura

manual car el coche con transmisión manual

map el mapa

market el mercado

married casado

marry v casarse

mass (church service) la misa

massage el masaje

match la cerilla

meal la comida

measure v **(someone)** medir

measuring cup la taza medidora

measuring spoon la cuchara medidora

mechanic el mecánico

medicine el medicamento

medium (size) mediano

meet v **(someone)** conocer

meeting la reunión; **~ room** la sala de reuniones

membership card la tarjeta de socio

memorial (place) el monumento conmemorativo

memory card la tarjeta de memoria

mend v zurcir

menstrual cramps los dolores menstruales

menu la carta

message el mensaje

meter (parking) el parquímetro

microwave el microondas

midday [BE] el mediodía

midnight la medianoche

mileage el kilometraje

mini-bar el minibar

minute el minuto

missing desaparecido

mistake el error

mobile móvil; **~ home** la caravana; **~ phone** [BE] el teléfono móvil

mobility la movilidad

money el dinero

month el mes

mop la fregona

moped el ciclomotor

more más

morning la mañana

mosque la mezquita

mother la madre

motion sickness el mareo

motor el motor; **~ boat** la lancha motora; **~cycle** la motocicleta; **~way** [BE] la autopista

mountain la montaña; **~ bike** la bicicleta de montaña

mousse (hair) la espuma para el pelo

mouth *n* la boca

movie la película; **~ theater** el cine

mug *v* asaltar

muscle (body part) el músculo

museum el museo

music la música; **~ store** la tienda de música

N

nail la uña; **~ file** la lima de uñas; **~ salon** el salon de manicura

name el nombre

napkin la servilleta

nappy [BE] el pañale

nationality la nacionalidad

nature preserve la reserva natural

(be) nauseous *v* tener náuseas

near cerca; **~-sighted** miope; **~by** cerca de aquí

neck el cuello

necklace el collar

need *v* necesitar

newspaper el periódico

newsstand el quiosco

next próximo

nice *adj* amable

night la noche; **~club** la discoteca

no no

non sin; **~-alcoholic** sin alcohol; **~-smoking** para no fumadores

noon el mediodía

north el norte

nose la nariz

note [BE] el billete

nothing nada

notify *v* avisar

novice (skill level) principiante

now ahora

number el número

nurse el enfermero/la enfermera

O

office la oficina; **~ hours (doctor's)** las horas de consulta; **~ hours (other offices)** el horario de oficina

off-licence [BE] la tienda de bebidas alcohólicas

oil el aceite

OK de acuerdo

old *adj* viejo

on the corner en la esquina

once una vez

one uno; **~-way ticket** el billete de ida; **~-way street** la calle de sentido único

only solamente

open *v* abrir; **~** *adj* abierto

opera la ópera; **~ house** el teatro de la ópera

opposite frente a

optician el oculista

orange (color) naranja

orchestra la orquesta

order *v* pedir

outdoor pool la piscina exterior

outside fuera

over sobre; **~ the counter (medication)** sin receta; **~look (scenic place)** el mirador; **~night** por la noche

oxygen treatment la oxigenoterapia

P

p.m. de la tarde

pacifier el chupete

pack *v* hacer las maletas

package el paquete

paddling pool [BE] la piscina infantil

pad [BE] la compresa

pain el dolor

pajamas los pijamas

palace el palacio

pants los pantalones

pantyhose las medias

paper el papel; **~ towel** el papel de cocina

paracetamol [BE] el paracetamol

park *v* aparcar; **~** *n* el parque; **~ing garage** el párking; **~ing lot** el aparcamiento

parliament building el palacio de las

cortes

part (for car) la pieza; **~-time** a tiempo parcial

pass through *v* estar de paso

passenger el pasajero

passport el pasaporte; **~ control** el control de pasaportes

password la contraseña

pastry shop la pastelería

path el camino

pay *v* pagar; **~ phone** el teléfono público

peak (of a mountain) la cima

pearl la perla

pedestrian el peatón

pediatrician el pediatra

pedicure la pedicura

pen el bolígrafo

penicillin la penicilina

penis el pene

per por; **~ day** por día; **~ hour** por hora; **~ night** por noche; **~ week** por semana

perfume el perfume

period (menstrual) la regla; **~ (of time)** la época

permit *v* permitir

petite las tallas pequeñas

petrol la gasolina; **~ station** la gasolinera

pewter el peltre

pharmacy la farmacia
phone v
hacer una llamada;
~ n el teléfono; ~
call la llamada de
teléfono; ~ **card** la
tarjeta telefónica; ~
number el número
de teléfono
photo la foto;
~**copy** la fotocopia;
~**graphy** la foto-
grafía
pick up v (**some-
thing**) recoger
picnic area la zona
para picnic
piece el trozo
Pill (birth control) la
píldora
pillow la almohada
**personal identifica-
tion number
(PIN)** la clave
pink rosa
piste [BE] la pista; ~
map [BE] el mapa
de pistas
pizzeria la pizzería
place v (**a bet**) hacer
una apuesta
plane el avión
plastic wrap el film
transparente
plate el plato
**platform [BE]
(train)** el andén
platinum el platino
play v jugar; ~ n
(**theater**) la obra de
teatro; ~**ground** el
patio de recreo;
~**pen** el parque
please por favor

pleasure el placer
plunger el desa-
tascador
plus size la talla
grande
pocket el bolsillo
poison el veneno
poles (skiing) los
bastones
police la policía; ~
report el certificado
de la policía; ~ **sta-
tion** la comisaría
pond el estanque
pool la piscina
pop music la música
pop
portion la ración
post [BE] el correo;
~ **office** la oficina
de correos; ~**box**
[BE] el buzón de
correos; ~**card** la
tarjeta postal
pot la olla
pottery la cerámica
**pounds (British
sterling)** las libras
esterlinas
pregnant embarazada
prescribe v recetar
prescription la receta
press v (**cloth-
ing**) planchar
price el precio
print v imprimir
problem el problema
produce las frutas y
verduras; ~ **store** la
frutería y verdulería
prohibit v prohibir
pronounce v
pronunciar
public el público

pull v (**door sign**) tirar
purple morado
purse el bolso
push v (**door
sign**) empujar;
~**chair [BE]** el
cochecito de niño

Q
quality n la calidad
question la pregunta
quiet adj tranquilo

R
racetrack el circuito
de carreras
racket (sports) la
raqueta
**railway station
[BE]** la estación de
trenes
rain la lluvia;
~**coat** el chubas-
quero; ~**forest** el
bosque pluvial;
~**y** adv lluvioso
rap (music) el rap
rape v violar; ~ n la
violación
rash la erupción
cutánea
razor blade la hoja de
afeitar
reach v localizar
ready listo
real auténtico
receipt el recibo
receive v recibir
reception la recepción
recharge v recargar
recommend v
recomendar
recommendation la
recomendación

recycle v reciclar
red rojo
refrigerator n la
nevera
region la región
registered mail el
correo certificado
regular normal
relationship la
relación
rent v alquilar
rental car el coche de
alquiler
repair v arreglar
repeat v repetir
reservation la
reserva;
~ **desk** la taquilla
reserve v reservar
restaurant el
restaurante
restroom el servicio
retired jubilado
return v (**some-
thing**) devolver; ~ n
[BE] la ida y vuelta
rib (body part) la
costilla
right (direction) derecha; ~ **of way** prior-
idad de paso
ring el anillo
river n el río
road map el mapa de
carreteras
rob v atracar
robbed atracado
romantic romántico
room la habitación;
~ **key** la llave de
habitación; ~ **ser-
vice** el servicio de
habitaciones
round-trip ida y vuelta

route la ruta

rowboat la barca de remos

rubbish [BE] la basura; ~ **bag** [BE] la bolsa de basura

rugby el rugby

ruins las ruinas

rush la prisa

S

sad triste

safe *n* la caja fuerte; ~ *adj* seguro

sales tax el IVA

same mismo

sandals las sandalias

sanitary napkin la compresa

saucepan el cazo

sauna la sauna

save *v* (computer) guardar

savings (account) la cuenta de ahorro

scanner el escáner

scarf la bufanda

schedule *v* programar; ~ *n* el horario

school el colegio

science la ciencia

scissors las tijeras

sea el mar

seat el asiento

security la seguridad

see *v* ver

self-service el autoservicio

sell *v* vender

seminar el seminario

send *v* enviar

senior citizen jubilado

separated (marriage) -separado

serious serio

service (in a restaurant) el servicio

sexually transmitted disease (STD) la enfermedad de transmisión sexual

shampoo el champú

sharp afilado

shaving cream la crema de afeitar

sheet la sábana

ship *v* enviar

shirt la camisa

shoe store la zapatería

shoes los zapatos

shop *v* comprar

shopping ir de compras; ~ **area** la zona de compras; ~ **centre** [BE] el centro comercial; ~ **mall** el centro comercial

short corto; ~ **sleeves** las mangas cortas; ~**s** los pantalones cortos; ~**-sighted** [BE] miope

shoulder el hombro

show *v* enseñar

shower la ducha

shrine el santuario

sick enfermo

side el lado; ~ **dish** la guarnición; ~ **effect** el efecto secundario; ~ **order** la guarnición

sightsee *v* hacer turismo

sightseeing tour el recorrido turístico

sign *v* (name) firmar

silk la seda

silver la plata

single (unmarried) soltero; ~ **bed** la cama; ~ **prints** una copia; ~ **room** una habitación individual

sink el lavabo

sister la hermana

sit *v* sentarse

size la talla

skin la piel

skirt la falda

ski *v* esquiar; ~ *n* el esquí; ~ **lift** el telesquí

sleep *v* dormir; ~**er car** el coche cama; ~**ing bag** el saco de dormir

slice *v* cortar en rodajas

slippers las zapatillas

slower más despacio

slowly despacio

small pequeño

smaller más pequeño

smoke *v* fumar

smoking (area) la zona de fumadores

snack bar la cafetería

sneakers las zapatillas de deporte

snorkeling equipment el equipo de esnórquel

snow la nieve; ~**board** la tabla de snowboard; ~**shoe** la raqueta de nieve; ~**y** nevado

soap el jabón

soccer el fútbol

sock el calcetín

some alguno

soother [BE] el chupete

sore throat las anginas

sorry lo siento

south el sur

souvenir el recuerdo; ~ **store** la tienda de recuerdos

spa el centro de salud y belleza

Spain España

Spanish el español

spatula la espátula

speak *v* hablar

special (food) la especialidad de la casa

specialist (doctor) el especialista

specimen el ejemplar

speeding el exceso de velocidad

spell *v* deletrear

spicy picante

spine (body part) la columna vertebral

spoon la cuchara

sports los deportes; ~ **massage** el masaje deportivo

sporting goods store la tienda de deportes

sprain el esguince

square cuadrado; ~ **kilometer** el kilómetro cuadrado; ~ **meter** el metro cuadrado

stadium el estadio

stairs las escaleras
stamp v (a ticket) picar; ~ n (postage) el sello
start v empezar
starter [BE] el aperitivo
station la estación; **bus ~** la estación de autobuses; **gas ~** la gasolinera; **muster ~** [BE] el punto de reunión; **petrol ~** [BE] la gasolinera; **subway ~** el metro; **train ~** la estación de tren
statue la estatua
stay v quedarse
steal v robar
steep empinado
sterling silver la plata esterlina
sting el escozor
stolen robado
stomach el estómago; **~ache** el dolor de estómago
stop v pararse; ~ n la parada
storey [BE] la planta
stove el horno
straight recto
strange extraño
stream el arroyo
stroller el cochecito
student el estudiante
study v estudiar
stunning impresionante
subtitle el subtítulo
subway el metro; ~ **station** la estación

de metro
suit el traje
suitcase la maleta
sun el sol; **~block** el protector solar total; **~burn** la quemadura solar; **~glasses** las gafas de sol; **~ny** soleado; **~screen** el protector solar; **~stroke** la insolación
super (fuel) súper; **~market** el supermercado
surfboard la tabla de surf
surgical spirit [BE] el alcohol etílico
swallow v tragar
sweater el jersey
sweatshirt la sudadera
sweet (taste) dulce; **~s** [BE] los caramelos
swelling la hinchazón
swim v nadar; **~suit** el bañador
symbol (keyboard) el símbolo
synagogue la sinagoga

T

table la mesa
tablet (medicine) el comprimido
take v llevar; ~ **away** [BE] para llevar
tampon el tampón
tapas bar el bar de tapas
taste v probar

taxi el taxi
team el equipo
telephone el teléfono
temporary provisional
tennis el tenis
tent la tienda de campaña; **~ peg** la estaca; ~ **pole** el mástil
terminal (airport) la terminal
terracotta la terracotta
terrible terrible
text v (send a message) enviar un mensaje de texto; ~ n (message) el texto
thank v dar las gracias a; ~ **you** gracias
that eso
theater el teatro
there ahí
thief el ladrón
thigh el muslo
thirsty sediento
this esto
throat la garganta
ticket el billete; ~ **office** el despacho de billetes; **~ed passenger** el pasajero con billete
tie (clothing) la corbata
time el tiempo; **~table** [BE] el horario
tire la rueda
tired cansado
tissue el pañuelo de papel
tobacconist el estanco

today hoy
toe el dedo del pie; **~nail** la uña del pie
toilet [BE] el servicio; ~ **paper** el papel higiénico
tomorrow mañana
tongue la lengua
tonight esta noche
too demasiado
tooth el diente; **~brush** el cepillo de dientes; **~paste** la pasta de dientes
total (amount) el total
tough (food) duro
tourist el turista; ~ **information office** la oficina de turismo
tour el recorrido turístico
tow truck la grúa
towel la toalla
tower la torre
town la ciudad; ~ **hall** el ayuntamiento; ~ **map** el mapa de ciudad; ~ **square** la plaza
toy el juguete; ~ **store** la tienda de juguetes
track (train) el andén
traditional tradicional
traffic light el semáforo
trail la pista; ~ **map** el mapa de la pista
trailer el remolque
train el tren; ~ **station** la estación de tren

transfer *v* cambiar
translate *v* traducir
trash la basura
travel *v* viajar; ~
agency la agencia
de viajes; ~ **sick-
ness** el mareo;
**~er's check
[cheque BE]** el
cheque de viaje
tree el árbol
trim (hair cut) cor-
tarse las puntas
trip el viaje
trolley [BE] el carrito
trousers [BE] los
pantalones
T-shirt la camiseta
turn off *v* apagar
turn on *v* encender
TV la televisión
type *v* escribir a
máquina
tyre [BE] la rueda

U

**United Kingdom
(U.K.)** el Reino
Unido
**United States
(U.S.)** los Estados
Unidos
ugly feo
umbrella el paraguas
unattended de-
satendido
unconscious incon-
sciente
underground [BE] el
metro; ~ **station
[BE]** la estación
de metro
underpants [BE] los
calzoncillos

understand *v* entender
underwear la ropa
interior
university la
universidad
unleaded (gas) la
gasolina sin plomo
upper superior
urgent urgente
use *v* usar
username el nombre
de usuario
utensil el cubierto

V

vacancy la habitación
libre
vacation las
vacaciones
vaccination la vacuna
vacuum cleaner la
aspiradora
vaginal infection
la infección vaginal
valid validez
valley el valle
valuable valioso
VAT [BE] el IVA
vegetarian veg-
etariano
**vehicle registra-
tion** el registro del
coche
viewpoint [BE] el
mirador
village el pueblo
vineyard la viña
**visa (passport docu-
ment)** el visado
visit *v* visitar; ~**ing
hours** el horario
de visita
visually impaired la
persona con

discapacidad visual
vitamin la vitamina
V-neck el cuello
de pico
vomit *v* vomitar

W

wait *v* esperar;
~ *n* la espera;
~**ing room** la sala
de espera
waiter el camarero
waitress la camarera
wake *v* despertarse;
~~**up call** la lla-
mada despertador
walk *v* caminar; ~ *n*
la caminata; ~**ing
route** la ruta de
senderismo
wallet la cartera
warm *v* (**some-
thing**) calentar;
~ *adj* (**tempera-
ture**) calor
washing machine la
lavadora
watch el reloj
waterfall la cascada
weather el tiempo
week la semana;
~**end** el fin de se-
mana; ~**ly** semanal
welcome *v* acoger
well bien; ~-**rest-
ed** descansado
west el oeste
what (question) qué
wheelchair la silla de
ruedas; ~ **ramp** la
rampa para silla
de ruedas
**when (ques-
tion)** cuándo

**where (ques-
tion)** dónde
white blanco; ~
gold el oro blanco
who (question) quién
widowed viudo
wife la mujer
window la ventana; ~
case el escaparate
windsurfer el
surfista
wine list la carta
de vinos
wireless inalám-
brico; ~ **internet** el
acceso inalámbrico a
internet; ~ **internet
service** el servicio
inalámbrico a
internet; ~ **phone** el
teléfono móvil
with con
withdraw *v* retirar;
~**al (bank)** retirar
fondos
without sin
woman la mujer
wool la lana
work *v* trabajar
wrap *v* envolver
wrist la muñeca
write *v* escribir

Y

year el año
yellow amarillo
yes sí
yesterday ayer
young joven
youth hostel el
albergue juvenil

Z

zoo el zoológico

SPANISH–ENGLISH

A

a tiempo completo full-time
a tiempo parcial part-time
la abadía abbey
el abanico fan (souvenir)
abierto *adj* open
el abogado lawyer
abrazar *v* hug
el abrebotellas bottle opener
el abrelatas can opener
el abrigo coat
abrir *v* open
el abuelo grandparent
aburrido boring
acampar *v* camp
el acantilado cliff
el acceso access; **~ inalámbrico a internet** wireless internet; **~ para discapacitados** handicapped- (disabled-BE) accessible
el accidente accident
el aceite oil
aceptar *v* accept
acoger *v* welcome
acompañar a *v* join
la acupuntura acupuncture
el adaptador adapter
adicional extra
adiós goodbye
las aduanas customs
el aeropuerto airport

afilado sharp
la agencia agency; **~ de viajes** travel agency
agotado exhausted
el agua water; **~ caliente** hot water; **~ potable** drinking water
las aguas termales hot spring
ahí there
ahora now
el aire air, air pump; **~ acondicionado** air conditioning
el albergue hostel; **~ juvenil** youth hostel
alérgico allergic; **~ a la lactosa** lactose intolerant
algo anything
el algodón cotton
alguno some
alimentar *v* feed
el allanamiento de morada break-in (burglary)
la almohada pillow
el alojamiento accommodation
alquilar *v* rent [hire BE]; **el ~ de coches** car rental [hire BE]
alto high
amable nice
amarillo yellow
la ambulancia am-

bulance
el amigo friend
el amor *n* love
anémico anemic
la anestesia anesthesia
las anginas sore throat
el anillo ring
el animal animal
antes de before
el antibiótico antibiotic
el año year
apagar *v* turn off
el aparcamiento parking lot [car park BE]
aparcar *v* park
el apartamento apartment
el apéndice appendix (body part)
el aperitivo appetizer [starter BE]
aquí here
el árbol tree
la aromaterapia aromatherapy
arreglar *v* repair
el arroyo stream
la arteria artery
la articulación joint (body part)
los artículos goods; **~ para el hogar** household good
la artritis arthritis

asaltar *v* mug
el asalto attack
el ascensor elevator [lift BE]
asiático Asian
el asiento seat; **~ de niño** car seat; **~ de pasillo** aisle seat
asistir *v* attend
asmático asthmatic
la aspiradora vacuum cleaner
la aspirina aspirin
atracado robbed
atracar *v* rob
Australia Australia
australiano Australian
auténtico real
el autobús bus; **~ rápido** express bus
automático automatic
la autopista highway [motorway BE]
el autoservicio self-service
la avería breakdown
el avión airplane, plane
avisar *v* notify
ayer yesterday
la ayuda *n* help
ayudar *v* help
el ayuntamiento town hall
azul blue

B

bailar *v* dance
bajarse *v* get off (a train, bus, subway)

bajo low
el ballet ballet
el baloncesto basketball
el bálsamo para después del afeitado aftershave
el banco bank
el bañador swimsuit
el baño bathroom
el bar bar; **~ de tapas** tapas bar; **~ gay** gay bar
barato cheap, inexpensive
la barbacoa barbecue
la barca de remos rowboat
el barco boat
los bastones poles (skiing)
la basura trash [rubbish BE]
la batería battery (car)
el bebé baby
beber v drink
la bebida n drink
beis beige
el béisbol baseball
besar v kiss
el biberón baby bottle
la biblioteca library
la bicicleta bicycle; **~ de montaña** mountain bike
el billete n bill (money); **~** ticket; **~ de autobús** bus ticket; **~ de ida** one-way (ticket); **~ de ida y vuelta** round trip [return BE]; **~ electrónico** e-ticket

el biquini bikini
blanco white
la blusa blouse
la boca mouth
el bolígrafo pen
la bolsa de basura garbage [rubbish BE] bag
el bolsillo pocket
el bolso purse [handbag BE]
los bomberos fire department
la bombilla lightbulb
borrar v clear (on an ATM); **~** v delete (computer)
el bosque forest; **~ pluvial** rainforest
las botas boots; **~ de montaña** hiking boots
el bote jar
la botella bottle
el brazo arm
británico British
el broche brooch
bucear to dive
bueno adj good
buenas noches good evening
buenas tardes good afternoon
buenos días good morning
la bufanda scarf
el buzón de correo mailbox [postbox BE]

C

la cabaña cabin (house)
el cabaré cabaret

la cabeza head (body part)
la cafetería cafe, coffee shop, snack bar
la caja case (amount); **~ fuerte** n safe
el cajero cashier; **~ automático** ATM
el calcetín sock
la calefacción heater [heating BE]
calentar v heat, warm
la calidad quality
la calle de sentido único one-way street
calor hot, warm (temperature)
las calorías calories
los calzoncillos briefs [underpants BE] (clothing)
la cama single bed; **~ de matrimonio** double bed
la cámara camera; **~ digital** digital camera
la camarera waitress
el camarero waiter
el camarote cabin (ship)
cambiar v change, exchange, transfer
el cambio n change (money); **~ de divisas** currency exchange
caminar v walk
la caminata n walk
el camino path
la camisa shirt
la camiseta T-shirt
el cámping campsite

el campo field (sports); **~ de batalla** battleground; **~ de golf** golf course
Canadá Canada
canadiense Canadian
cancelar v cancel
el/la canguro babysitter
cansado tired
el cañón canyon
la cara face
los caramelos candy [sweets BE]
la caravana mobile home
el carbón charcoal
el carnicero butcher
caro expensive
el carrete film (camera)
el carrito cart [trolley BE] (grocery store); **~ de equipaje** luggage cart
la carta letter
la carta n menu; **~ de bebidas** drink menu; **~ para niños** children's menu; **~ de vinos** wine list
la cartera n wallet
el cartón carton; **~ de tabaco** carton of cigarettes
la casa house; **~ de cambio** currency exchange office
casado married
casarse v marry
la cascada waterfall
el casco helmet

los cascos headphones
el casino casino
el castillo castle
el catarro cold (sickness)
la catedral cathedral
el catre cot
causar daño v damage
el cazo saucepan
el CD CD
la cena dinner
el centímetro centimeter
el centro downtown area; ~ **comercial** shopping mall [centre BE]; ~ **de negocios** business center; ~ **de salud y belleza** spa
el cepillo de pelo hair brush
la cerámica pottery
cerca near; ~ **de aquí** nearby
la cerilla v match
cerrado closed
cerrar v close, lock; ~ **sesión** v log off (computer)
el cerrojo n lock
el certificado certificate; ~ **de la policía** police report
la cesta basket (grocery store)
el chaleco salvavidas life jacket
el champú shampoo
la chaqueta jacket
la charcutería delicatessen

el cheque n check [cheque BE] (payment); ~ **de viaje** traveler's check [cheque BE]
el chicle chewing gum
chino Chinese
el chubasquero raincoat
el chupete pacifier [soother BE]
el cibercafé internet cafe
el ciclismo cycling
el ciclomotor moped
la ciencia science
el cigarrillo cigarette
la cima peak (of a mountain)
el cine movie theater
la cinta transportadora conveyor belt
el cinturón n belt
el circuito de carreras racetrack
la cita appointment
la ciudad town
la clase class; ~ **económica** economy class; ~ **preferente** business class
la clave personal identification number (PIN)
el club de jazz jazz club
cobrar v bill (charge); ~ v cash; ~ v charge (credit card)
el cobre copper
el coche n car; ~ **de alquiler** rental [hire BE] car; ~ **automáti-**

co automatic car; ~ **cama** sleeper [sleeping BE] car; ~ **con transmisión manual** manual car
el cochecito stroller [pushchair BE]
la cocina kitchen
cocinar v cook
el código de país country code
el codo elbow
la colada laundry
el colegio school
la colina hill
el collar necklace
la colonia cologne
el color color
la columna vertebral spine (body part)
el comedor dining room
comer v eat
la comida food, lunch, meal; ~ **rápida** fast food
la comisaría police station
cómo how
el compañero de trabajo colleague
la compañía company; ~ **aérea** airline; ~ **de seguros** insurance company
comprar v buy, shop
la compresa sanitary napkin [pad BE]
el comprimido tablet (medicine)
con with; ~ **plomo** leaded (gas)
el concierto concert

conducir v drive
conectarse v connect (internet)
la conexión connection (internet); ~ **de vuelo** connection (flight)
la conferencia conference
confirmar v confirm
el congelador freezer
la congestión congestion
conocer v meet (someone)
la consigna automática luggage locker
el consulado Consulate
el consultor consultant
contagioso contagious
la contraseña password
el control de pasaportes passport control
el corazón heart
la corbata tie (clothing)
el correo n mail [post BE]; ~ **aéreo** airmail; ~ **certificado** registered mail; ~ **electrónico** n e-mail
cortar v cut (hair); ~ **en rodajas** to slice
cortarse las puntas v trim (hair cut)
el corte n cut (injury); ~ **de pelo** haircut
corto short

costar v cost

la costilla rib (body part)

la crema cream; **~ antiséptica** antiseptic cream; **~ de afeitar** shaving cream; **~ hidratante** lotion

el cristal crystal

el cruce intersection

cuándo when (question)

cuánto cuesta how much

el cubierto utensil

la cuchara spoon; **~ medidora** measuring spoon

la cucharadita teaspoon

la cuchilla desechable disposable razor

el cuchillo knife

el cuello neck; **~ de pico** V-neck; **~ redondo** crew neck

el cuenco bowl

la cuenta account; **~ de ahorro** savings account; **~ corriente** checking [current BE] account

cuero leather

la cueva cave

el cumpleaños birthday

la cuna crib

D

dar to give; **~ el pecho** breastfeed; **~ fuego** light (ciga-

rette); **~ las gracias a** v thank

de from, of; **~ acuerdo** OK; **~ la mañana** a.m.; **~ la tarde** p.m.; **~ la zona** local

declarar v declare

el dedo finger; **~ del pie** toe

deletrear v spell

delicioso delicious

la dentadura denture

el dentista dentist

dentro in

la depilacion wax; **~ de cejas** eyebrow wax; **~ de las ingles** bikini wax

deportes sports

depositar v deposit

el depósito bancario deposit (bank)

la derecha right (direction)

desaparecido missing

el desatascador plunger

desatendido unattended

el desayuno breakfast

descansado well-rested

desconectar v disconnect (computer)

el descuento discount

desechable disposable

el desierto desert

el desodorante deodorant

despachar medicamentos v fill [make up BE] a prescription

el despacho de billetes ticket office

despacio slowly

despertarse v wake

después after

el detergente detergent

detrás de behind (direction)

devolver v exchange, return (goods)

el día day

diabético diabetic

el diamante diamond

la diarrea diarrhea

el diente tooth

el diesel diesel

difícil difficult

digital digital

el dinero money

la dirección direction

la dirección address; **~ de correo electrónico** e-mail address

discapacitado handicapped [disabled BE]

la discoteca club (dance, night); **~ gay** gay club

disculparse v excuse (to get attention)

disfrutar v enjoy

disponible available

divorciar v divorce

doblada dubbed

doblando (la esquina) around (the corner)

la docena dozen

el documento de identidad identification

el dólar dollar (U.S.)

el dolor pain; **~ de cabeza** headache; **~ de espalda** backache; **~ de estómago** stomachache; **~ de oído** earache; **~ de pecho** chest pain

los dolores menstruales menstrual cramps

dónde where (question)

dormir v sleep

el dormitorio dormitory

la ducha shower

dulce sweet (taste)

durante during

el DVD DVD

E

la edad age

el edificio building

el efectivo cash

el efecto secundario side effect

el ejemplar specimen

embarazada pregnant

embarcar v board

la emergencia emergency

el empaste filling (tooth)

empezar v begin, start

empinado steep

empujar v push (door sign)

en la esquina on the corner

el encaje lace

encender v turn on

el enchufe eléctrico electric outlet

encontrarse mal *v* be ill

la enfermedad de transmisión sexual sexually transmitted disease (STD)

el enfermero/la enfermera nurse

enfermo sick

enseñar *v* show

entender *v* understand

la entrada admission/cover charge; **~ entrance**

entrar *v* enter

el entretenimiento entertainment

enviar *v* send, ship; **~ por correo** *v* mail; **~ un correo electrónico** *v* e-mail; **~ un fax** *v* fax; **~ un mensaje de texto** *v* text (send a message)

envolver *v* wrap

la época period (of time)

el equipaje luggage [baggage BE]; **~ de mano** carry-on (piece of hand luggage)

el equipo team

el equipo equipment; **~ de buceo** diving equipment; **~ de esnórquel** snorkeling equipment

equis ele (XL) extra large

el error mistake

la erupción cutánea rash

las escaleras stairs; **~ mecánicas** escalators

el escáner scanner

el escaparate window case

la escoba broom

el escozor sting

escribir *v* write; **~ a máquina** *v* type

el escurridor colander

el esguince sprain

el esmalte enamel (jewelry)

eso that

la espalda back

España Spain

el español Spanish

la espátula spatula

la especialidad de la casa special (food)

el especialista specialist (doctor)

la espera *n* wait

esperar *v* wait

la espuma para el pelo mousse (hair)

el esquí *n* ski

esquiar *v* ski

los esquís acuáticos water skis

esta noche tonight

la estaca tent peg

la estación station; **~ de autobuses** bus station; **~ de metro** subway [underground BE] station; **~ de tren** train [railway BE] station

el estadio stadium

el estado de salud condition (medical)

los Estados Unidos United States (U.S.)

estadounidense American

el estanco tobacconist

el estanque pond

estar *v* be; **~ de paso** *v* pass through

la estatua statue

el este east

el estilista hairstylist

esto this

el estómago stomach

estreñido constipated

estrellarse *v* crash (car)

estudiando studying

el estudiante student

estudiar *v* study

el euro euro

el exceso excess; **~ de velocidad** speeding

la excursión excursion

experto expert (skill level)

la extensión extension (phone)

extraer *v* extract (tooth)

extraño strange

F

fácil *adj* easy

la factura bill [invoice BE]

la facturación check-in (airport)

facturar check (luggage)

la falda skirt

la familia family

la farmacia pharmacy [chemist BE]

el fax *n* fax

la fecha date (calendar)

feliz *adj* happy

feo *adj* ugly

el ferry ferry

la fianza deposit (to reserve a room)

la fiebre fever

el film transparente plastic wrap [cling film BE]

el fin de semana weekend

firmar *v* sign (name)

la flor flower

la fórmula infantil formula (baby)

el formulario form

la foto exposure (film); **~ photo; ~copia** photocopy; **~grafía** photography; **~ digital** digital photo

la fregona mop

los frenos brakes (car)

frente a opposite

fresco fresh

frío *adj* cold (temperature)

las frutas y verduras produce

la frutería y verdulería produce store

el fuego fire

la fuente fountain

fuera outside

el fuerte fort

fumar *v* smoke

la funda para la cámara camera case

el fútbol soccer [football BE]

G

las gafas glasses; **~ de sol** sunglasses

el garaje garage (parking)

la garganta throat

la garrafa carafe

el gas butano cooking gas

la gasolina gas [petrol BE]; **~ sin plomo** unleaded gas

la gasolinera gas [petrol BE] station

gay gay

el gerente manager

el gimnasio gym

el ginecólogo gynecologist

la gomina gel (hair)

la gota drop (medicine)

grabar v burn (CD); **~** v engrave

gracias thank you

los grados degrees (temperature); **~ centígrado** Celsius

el gramo gram

grande large

los grandes almacenes department store

la granja farm

gratuito free

gris gray

la grúa tow truck

el grupo group

guapo attractive

guardar v save (computer)

la guarnición side dish, order

el guía guide

la guía guide book; **~ de tiendas** store directory

gustar v like; **me gusta** I like

H

ha sufrido daños damaged

la habitación room; **~ individual** single room; **~ libre** vacancy

hablar v speak

hacer v have; **~ una apuesta** v place (a bet); **~ un arreglo** v alter; **~ una llamada** v phone; **~ las maletas** v pack; **~ turismo** sightseeing

hambriento hungry

helado icy

la hermana sister

el hermano brother

el hielo ice

el hígado liver (body part)

la hinchazón swelling

hipermétrope farsighted [long-sighted BE]

el hipódromo horsetrack

el hockey hockey; **~ sobre hielo** ice hockey

la hoja de afeitar razor blade

hola hello

el hombre man

el hombro shoulder

hondo deeply

la hora hour

el horario n schedule [timetable BE]

los horarios hours; **~ de atención al público** business hours; **~ de oficina** office hours; **~ de visita** visiting hours

las horas de consulta office hours (doctor's)

el hornillo camp stove

el horno stove

el hospital hospital

el hotel hotel

hoy today

el hueso bone

I

el ibuprofeno ibuprofen

la ida y vuelta round-trip [return BE]

la iglesia church

impresionante stunning

imprimir v print

el impuesto duty (tax)

incluir v include

inconsciente unconscious

increíble amazing

la infección vaginal vaginal infection

infectado infected

el inglés English

iniciar sesión v log on (computer)

el insecto bug

la insolación sunstroke

el insomnio insomnia

la insulina insulin

interesante interesting

internacional international (airport area)

la internet internet

el/la intérprete interpreter

el intestino intestine

introducir v insert

ir a v go (somewhere)

ir de compras v go shopping

Irlanda Ireland

irlandés Irish

el IVA sales tax [VAT BE]

la izquierda left (direction)

J

el jabón soap

el jardín botánico botanical garden

el jazz jazz

el jersey sweater

joven young

las joyas jewelry

la joyería jeweler

jubilado retired

jugar v play

el juguete toy

K

el kilo kilo; **~gramo** kilogram; **~metraje** mileage

el **kilómetro** kilometer; ~ **cuadrado** square kilometer

L

el **labio** lip
la **laca** hairspray
el **ladrón** thief
el **lago** lake
la **lana** wool
la **lancha motora** motor boat
largo long
el **lavabo** sink
la **lavadora** washing machine
la **lavandería** laundromat [launderette BE]
lavar v wash
el **lavavajillas** dishwasher
la **lección** lesson
lejos far
la **lengua** tongue
la **lente** lens
las **lentillas de contacto** contact lens
las **letras** arts
las **libras esterlinas** pounds (British sterling)
libre de impuestos duty-free
la **librería** bookstore
el **libro** book
la **lima de uñas** nail file
limpiar v clean
la **limpieza de cutis** facial
limpio adj clean
la **línea** line (train)
el **lino** linen
la **linterna** flashlight

el **líquido** liquid; ~ **de lentillas de contacto** contact lens solution; ~ **lavavajillas** dishwashing liquid
listo ready
la **litera** berth
el **litro** liter
la **llamada** n call; ~ **de teléfono** phone call; ~ **despertador** wake-up call
llamar v call
la **llave** key; ~ **de habitación** room key; ~ **electrónica** key card
el **llavero** key ring
las **llegadas** arrivals (airport)
llegar v arrive
llenar v fill
llevar v take; ~ **en coche** lift (to give a ride)
la **lluvia** rain
lluvioso rainy
lo siento sorry
localizar v reach
la **luz** light (overhead)

M

la **madre** mother
magnífico magnificent
el **malestar estomacal** upset stomach
la **maleta** bag, suitcase
la **mandíbula** jaw
las **mangas cortas** short sleeves
las **mangas**

largas long sleeves
la **manicura** manicure
la **mano** hand
la **manta** blanket
mañana tomorrow; la ~ morning
el **mapa** map; ~ **de carreteras** road map; ~ **de ciudad** town map; ~ **de la pista** trail [piste BE] map
el **mar** sea
marcar v dial
mareado dizzy
el **mareo** motion [travel BE] sickness
el **marido** husband
marrón brown
el **martillo** hammer
más more; ~ **alto** louder; ~ **bajo** lower; ~ **barato** cheaper; ~ **despacio** slower; ~ **grande** larger; ~ **pequeño** smaller; ~ **rápido** faster; ~ **tarde** later; ~ **temprano** earlier
el **masaje** massage; ~ **deportivo** sports massage
el **mástil** tent pole
el **mecánico** mechanic
el **mechero** lighter
la **media hora** half hour
mediano medium (size)
la **medianoche** midnight
el **medicamento** medicine

el **médico** doctor
medio half; ~ **kilo** half-kilo; ~ **día** noon [midday BE]
medir v measure (someone)
mejor best
menos less
el **mensaje** message; ~ **instantáneo** instant message
el **mes** month
la **mesa** table
el **metro** subway [underground BE]
el **metro cuadrado** square meter
la **mezquita** mosque
el **microondas** microwave
el **minibar** mini-bar
el **minuto** minute
el **mirador** overlook [viewpoint BE] (scenic place)
mirar v look
la **misa** mass (church service)
mismo same
los **mocasines** loafers
la **mochila** backpack
molestar v bother
la **moneda** coin, currency
mono cute
la **montaña** n mountain
el **monumento conmemorativo** memorial (place)
morado purple

el mostrador de información information desk
mostrar v display
la moto acuática jet ski
la motocicleta motorcycle
movilidad mobility
la mujer wife, woman
la multa fine (fee for breaking law)
la muñeca doll; ~ wrist
el músculo muscle
el museo museum
la música music; ~ **clásica** classical music; ~ **folk** folk music; ~ **pop** pop music
el muslo thigh

N

nacional domestic
la nacionalidad nationality
nada nothing
nadar v swim
las nalgas buttocks
naranja orange (color)
la nariz nose
necesitar v need
los negocios business
negro black
nevado snowy
la nevera refrigerator
el nieto grandchild
la niña girl
el niño boy, child
el nivel intermedio intermediate
no no
la noche evening, night
el nombre name; ~ **de usuario** username
normal regular
las normas de vestuario dress code
el norte north
la novia girlfriend
el novio boyfriend
el número number; ~ **de fax** fax number; ~ **de permiso de conducir** driver's license number; ~ **de teléfono** phone number; ~ **de teléfono de información** information (phone)

O

la obra de teatro n play (theater)
el oculista optician
el oeste west
la oficina office; ~ **de correos** post office; ~ **de objetos perdidos** lost and found; ~ **de turismo** tourist information office
el ojo eye
la olla pot
la ópera opera
el ordenador computer
la oreja ear
la orina urine
el oro gold; ~ **amarillo** yellow gold; ~ **blanco** white gold
la orquesta orchestra

oscuro dark
el otro camino alternate route
la oxigenoterapia oxygen treatment

P

padecer del corazón heart condition
el padre father
pagar v pay
el pájaro bird
el palacio palace; ~ **de las cortes** parliament building
los palillos chinos chopsticks
la panadería bakery
los pantalones pants [trousers BE]; ~ **cortos** shorts
el pañal diaper [nappy BE]
el pañuelo de paper tissue
el papel paper; ~ **de aluminio** aluminum [kitchen BE] foil; ~ **de cocina** paper towel; ~ **higiénico** toilet paper
el paquete package
para for; ~ **llevar** to go (take away BE); ~ **no fumadores** non-smoking
el paracetamol acetaminophen [paracetamol BE]
la parada n stop; ~ **de autobús** bus stop
el paraguas umbrella

pararse v stop
el párking parking garage
el parque playpen; ~ park; ~ **de atracciones** amusement park
el partido game; ~ **de fútbol** soccer [football BE]; ~ **de voleibol** volleyball game
el pasajero passenger; ~ **con billete** ticketed passenger
el pasaporte passport
el pase de acceso a los remontes lift pass
el pasillo aisle
la pasta de dientes toothpaste
la pastelería pastry shop
el patio de recreo playground
el peatón pedestrian
el pecho chest (body part)
el pediatra pediatrician
la pedicura pedicure
pedir v order
el peinado hairstyle
el peine comb
la película movie
peligroso dangerous
el pelo hair
el peltre pewter
la peluquería de caballeros barber
la peluquería hair salon

los pendientes earrings

el pene penis

la penicilina penicillin

la pensión bed and breakfast

pequeño small

perder v lose (something)

perdido lost

el perfume perfume

el periódico newspaper

la perla pearl

permitir v allow, permit

el perro guía guide dog

la persona con discapacidad visual visually impaired person

la picadura de insecto insect bite

picante spicy

picar v stamp (a ticket)

el pie foot

la piel skin

la pierna leg

la pieza part (for car)

los pijamas pajamas

la pila battery

la píldora Pill (birth control)

la piscina pool; ~ **cubierta** indoor pool; ~ **exterior** outdoor pool; ~ **infantil** kiddie [paddling BE] pool

la pista trail [piste BE]

la pizzería pizzeria

el placer pleasure

la plancha n iron (clothes)

planchar v iron

la planta floor [storey BE]; ~ **baja** ground floor

la plata silver; ~ **esterlina** sterling silver

el platino platinum

el plato dish (kitchen); ~ **principal** main course

la playa beach

la plaza town square

la policía police

la pomada cream (ointment)

ponerse en contacto con v contact

por for; ~ per; ~ **día** per day; ~ **favor** please; ~ **hora** per hour; ~ **la noche** overnight; ~ **noche** per night; ~ **semana** per week

el postre dessert

el precio price

precioso beautiful

el prefijo area code

la pregunta question

presentar v introduce

el preservativo condom

la primera clase first class

primero first

los principales sitios de interés main attraction

principiante beginner, novice (skill level)

la prioridad de paso right of way

la prisa rush

el probador fitting room

probar v taste

el problema problem

el producto good; ~ **de limpieza** cleaning product

programar v schedule

prohibir v prohibit

el pronóstico forecast

pronunciar v pronounce

el protector solar sunscreen

provisional temporary

próximo next

el público public

el pueblo village

el puente bridge

la puerta gate (airport); ~ door; ~ **de incendios** fire door

el pulmón lung

la pulsera bracelet

el puro cigar

Q

qué what (question)

quedar bien v fit (clothing)

quedarse v stay

la queja complaint

la quemadura solar sunburn

querer v love (someone)

quién who (question)

el quiosco newsstand

R

la ración portion; ~ **para niños** children's portion

la rampa para silla de ruedas wheelchair ramp

el rap rap (music)

rápido express, fast

la raqueta racket (sports); ~ **de nieve** snowshoe

la reacción alérgica allergic reaction

recargar v recharge

la recepción reception

la receta prescription

recetar v prescribe

rechazar v decline (credit card)

recibir v receive

el recibo receipt

reciclar v recycling

recoger v pick up (something)

la recogida de equipajes baggage claim

la recomendación recommendation

recomendar v recommend

el recorrido tour; ~ **en autobús** bus tour; ~ **turístico** sightseeing tour

recto straight

el recuerdo souvenir

el regalo gift

la región region

el registro check-in (hotel); ~ **del coche** vehicle registration

la regla period (menstrual)

el Reino Unido United Kingdom (U.K.)

la relación relationship

rellenar v fill out (form)

el reloj watch; **~ de pared** wall clock

el remolque trailer

reparar v fix (repair)

el repelente de insectos insect repellent

repetir v repeat

la resaca hangover

la reserva reservation; **~ natural** nature preserve

reservar v reserve

el/la residente de la UE EU resident

respirar v breathe

el restaurante restaurant

retirar v withdraw; **~ fondos** withdrawal (bank)

retrasarse v delay

la reunión meeting

revelar v develop (film)

revisar v check (on something)

la revista magazine

el riñón kidney (body part)

el río river

robado stolen

robar v steal

el robo theft

la rodilla knee

rojo red

romántico romantic

romper v break

la ropa clothing; **~ interior** underwear

rosa pink

roto broken

el rugby rugby

la rueda tire (tyre BE); **~ pinchada** flat tire (tyre BE)

las ruinas ruins

la ruta route; **~ de senderismo** walking route

S

la sábana sheet

el sacacorchos corkscrew

el saco de dormir sleeping bag

la sala room; **~ de conciertos** concert hall; **~ de espera** waiting room; **~ de reuniones** meeting room

la salida check-out (hotel)

la salida n exit; **~ de urgencia** emergency exit

las salidas departures (airport)

salir v exit, leave

el salón room; **~ de congresos** convention hall; **~ de juegos recreativos** arcade; **~ de manicura** nail salon

¡Salud! Cheers!

la salud health

las sandalias sandals

sangrar v bleed

la sangre blood

el santuario shrine

la sartén frying pan

la sauna sauna

el secador de pelo hair dryer

la secreción discharge (bodily fluid)

la seda silk

sediento thirsty

la seguridad security

el seguro insurance

seguro safe (protected)

el sello n stamp (postage)

el semáforo traffic light

la semana week

semanal weekly

el seminario seminar

el sendero trail; **~ para bicicletas** bike route

el seno breast

sentarse v sit

separado separated (marriage)

ser v be

serio serious

el servicio restroom (toilet BE]; **~** service (in a restaurant); **~ completo** full-service; **~ de habitaciones** room service; **~ inalámbrico a internet** wireless internet service; **~ de internet** internet service; **~ de lavandería** laundry service; **~ de limpieza de habitaciones** housekeeping service

la servilleta napkin

sí yes

el sida AIDS

la silla chair; **~ para niños** child seat; **~ de ruedas** wheelchair

el símbolo symbol (keyboard)

sin without; **~ alcohol** non-alcoholic; **~ grasa** fat free; **~ receta** over the counter (medication)

la sinagoga synagogue

el sitio de interés attraction (place)

el sobre envelope

el socorrista lifeguard

el sol sun

solamente only

soleado sunny

solo alone

soltero single (marriage)

el sombrero hat

la somnolencia drowsiness

sordo deaf

soso bland

el suavizante conditioner

el subtítulo subtitle

sucio dirty

la sudadera sweatshirt

el suelo floor

el sujetador bra

súper super (fuel)

superior upper
el supermer-
cado grocery store,
supermarket
la supervisión su-
pervision
el sur south
el surfista windsurfer

T

la tabla board; ~
de snowboard
snowboard; ~ **de**
surf surfboard
la talla size; ~
grande plus size; ~
pequeña petite size
el taller garage
(repair)
el talón de
equipaje luggage
[baggage BE] ticket
el tampón tampon
la taquilla locker; ~
reservation desk
tarde late (time)
la tarde afternoon
la tarjeta card;
~ **de cajero**
automático ATM
card; ~ **de crédi-**
to credit card;
~ **de débito** debit
card; ~ **de em-**
barque board-
ing pass; ~ **interna-**
cional de estudiante
international student
card; ~ **de memo-**
ria memory card;
~ **de nego-**
cios business card;
~ **postal** postcard;
~ **de seguro**

insurance card;
~ **de socio**
membership card;
~ **telefónica**
phone card
la tasa fee
el taxi taxi
la taza cup; ~ **medi-**
dora measuring cup
el teatro theater; ~
de la ópera opera
house
la tela imperme-
able groundcloth
[groundsheet BE]
el teleférico cable car
el teléfono telephone;
~ **móvil** cell
[mobile BE] phone;
~ **público** pay
phone
la telesilla chair lift
el telesquí ski/
drag lift
la televisión TV
el templo temple
(religious)
temprano early
el tenedor fork
tener v have; ~
dolor v hurt (have
pain); ~ **náuseas** v
be nauseous
el tenis tennis
la tensión arte-
rial blood pressure
la terminal terminal
(airport)
terminar v end
la terracotta ter-
racotta
terrible terrible
el texto n text
(message)

el tiempo time;
~ **weather**
la tienda store;
~ **de alimentos**
naturales health
food store; ~ **de an-**
tigüedades an-
tique store; ~ **de**
bebidas alcohólicas
liquor store [off-
licence BE]; ~ **de**
campaña tent; ~ **de**
deportes sporting
goods store; ~ **de**
fotografía cam-
era store; ~ **de**
juguetes toy store;
~ **de música** music
store; ~ **de recuer-**
dos souvenir store;
~ **de rega-**
los gift shop;
~ **de ropa** clothing
store
las tijeras scissors
la tintorería dry
cleaner
el tipo de cambio ex-
change rate
tirar v pull (door sign)
la tirita bandage
la toalla towel
la toallita baby wipe
el tobillo ankle
el torneo de golf golf
tournament
la torre tower
la tos n cough
toser v cough
el total total (amount)
trabajar v work
tradicional traditional
traducir v translate
traer v bring

tragar v swallow
el traje suit
tranquilo quiet
el tren train; ~
rápido express train
triste sad
la trona highchair
el trozo piece
la tumbona deck
chair
el/la turista tourist

U

último last
la universidad uni-
versity
uno one
la uña nail; ~ **del**
dedo fingernail;
~ **del pie** toenail
urgente urgent
usar v use

V

las vacaciones vaca-
tion [holiday BE]
vaciar v empty
la vacuna vaccination
la vagina vagina
la validez valid
valioso valuable
el valle valley
el valor value
el vaquero denim
los vaqueros jeans
el vaso glass
(drinking)
el váter quími-
co chemical toilet
vegetariano veg-
etarian
la vejiga bladder
vender v sell
el veneno poison

venir v come
la ventana window
el ventilador fan
(appliance)
ver v see
verde green
el vestido dress (piece
of clothing)
el viaje trip
el vidrio glass
(material)

viejo old
la viña vineyard
la violación n rape
violar v rape
el visado visa (pass-
port document)
visitar v visit
la vitamina vitamin
la vitrina display case
viudo widowed
vivir v live

vomitar v vomit
el vuelo flight; **~
internacional**
international flight; **~
nacional** domestic
flight

Z

la zapatería shoe
store
las zapatillas slip-

pers; **~ de de-
porte** sneaker
los zapatos shoes
la zona area; **~ de
compras** shopping
area; **~ de fuma-
dores** smoking area;
~ para picnic picnic
area
el zoológico zoo
zurcir v mend

INDEX

Berlitz pocket guide

ANDALUCÍA & THE COSTA DEL SOL

Fifteenth Edition 2018

Editor: Carine Tracanelli
Author: Norman Renouf, Nick Inman, Clara Villanueva
Head of Production: Rebeka Davies
Picture Editor: Tom Smyth
Cartography Update: Carte
Update Production: Apa Digital
Photography Credits: 123RF 75; Corrie Wingate/Apa Publications 4MC, 4ML, 5MC, 5MC, 6L, 15, 16, 19, 25, 28, 31, 63, 64, 69, 70, 72, 76, 79, 80, 89, 93, 97, 98, 101, 103, 104; Dreamstime 4TC, 5M, 5TC, 20, 33, 35, 45, 55, 84, 94; iStock 4TL, 5T, 6R, 7R, 11, 13, 37, 38, 42, 49, 51, 56, 59, 60, 83, 86, 90; Mark Read/Apa Publications 87; PGHCOM 22; Shutterstock 5M, 7, 39, 41, 47, 53, 67; SuperStock 1
Cover Picture: iStock

Distribution
UK, Ireland and Europe: Apa Publications (UK) Ltd; sales@insightguides.com
United States and Canada: Ingram Publisher Services; ips@ingramcontent.com
Australia and New Zealand: Woodslane; info@woodslane.com.au
Southeast Asia: Apa Publications (SN) Pte; singaporeoffice@insightguides.com
Worldwide: Apa Publications (UK) Ltd; sales@insightguides.com

Special Sales, Content Licensing and CoPublishing
Insight Guides can be purchased in bulk quantities at discounted prices. We can create special editions, personalised jackets and corporate imprints tailored to your needs. sales@insightguides.com; www.insightguides.biz

All Rights Reserved
© 2018 Apa Digital (CH) AG and Apa Publications (UK) Ltd

Printed in China by CTPS

No part of this book may be reproduced, stored in a retrieval system or transmitted in any form or means electronic, mechanical, photocopying, recording or otherwise, without prior written permission from Apa Publications.

Contact us
Every effort has been made to provide accurate information in this publication, but changes are inevitable. The publisher cannot be responsible for any resulting loss, inconvenience or injury. We would appreciate it if readers would call our attention to any errors or outdated information. We also welcome your suggestions; please contact us at: berlitz@apaguide.co.uk www.insightguides.com/berlitz

Berlitz Trademark Reg. U.S. Patent Office and other countries. Marca Registrada. Used under licence from the Berlitz Investment Corporation